THE YOUNG MELBOURNE

WILLIAM LAMB afterwards 2nd Viscount Melbourne
*From a painting by Sir Thomas Lawrence in the possession of the
Dowager Viscountess Hambleden*

DAVID CECIL

The Young
MELBOURNE

*And the Story of His Marriage
with Caroline Lamb*

THE BOBBS-MERRILL COMPANY
Publishers

INDIANAPOLIS   NEW YORK

Printed in the United States of America

PRINTED AND BOUND BY
BRAUNWORTH & CO., INC.
BUILDERS OF BOOKS
BRIDGEPORT, CONN.

To
Rachel Cecil

PREFATORY NOTE

A WELL-EXECUTED design should need no elucidation. But the nature of my subject has involved me in certain peculiarities of treatment which may justify me in offering a few sentences of explanation. My book is a study in the evolution of a character, William Lamb, Lord Melbourne's. His was a complex nature slow to develop; it was not until middle-age that it reached full maturity. I trace his story therefore until the age of forty-seven, just before the opening of his active career as a public man. The book is divided into three parts, corresponding to the three main stages in his development; and closes with an analysis, illustrated by references both to his earlier and subsequent life, of his character at last set into that final shape, in which it made its mark on history. Further during these formative years he was a passive figure. His story is mainly the story of the influence exerted on his spirit by other characters, and their activities. To understand him, we must understand them. My picture in consequence is not so much a single portrait as a conversation piece.

I must add some words of gratitude: first to His Majesty the King, for graciously permitting me to consult

PREFATORY NOTE

the archives at Windsor Castle, and to reproduce a portrait from the collection there: to Lady Desborough, the Dowager Lady Hambleden, Lord Crewe, Lord Spencer, Lord Leconfield and Sir John Murray for allowing me to reproduce other portraits; to Sir John Murray again for permitting me to quote from the correspondence of Lord Granville Leveson-Gower; to Lady Desborough, the Duke of Devonshire, Lord Ilchester and Lord Bessborough for allowing me to make use of their private papers; and to Sir Edward Marsh for correcting my proofs. If I have failed in my attempt to re-create a vanished age for the entertainment of my readers, I cannot plead that it is for lack of assistance.

DAVID CECIL.

CONTENTS

ILLUSTRATIONS

ILLUSTRATIONS

CHIEF EVENTS

1779 Birth of William Lamb.

1785 Birth of Caroline Ponsonby.

1790 William goes to Eton.

1796 William goes to Cambridge.

1799 William takes his degree.
       William goes to Glasgow to study.

1804 William admitted to the Bar.

1805 Peniston Lamb dies.
       William marries Caroline Ponsonby.

1806 William M.P. for Leominster.

1807 Augustus Lamb born.

1812 Caroline Lamb meets Byron.
       William retires from Parliament.

1813 Lady Heathcote's ball.

1815 The Lambs visit Brussels and Paris.

1816 William M.P. for Northampton.
       Glenarvon published.

1819 William M.P. for Hertford.

1825 William separates from Caroline.

1826 William retires from his Hertford seat.

1828 Death of Caroline Lamb.

THE GREAT Whig country houses of the eighteenth and early nineteenth centuries are among the most conspicuous monuments of English history. Ornate and massive, with their pedimented porticoes, their spreading balustraded wings, they dominate the landscape round them with a magnificent self-assurance. Nor are their interiors less imposing. Their colonnaded entrance halls, whence the Adam staircase sweeps up beneath a fluted dome; their cream and gilt libraries piled with sumptuous editions of the classics; their orangeries peopled with casts from the antique; their saloons hung with yellow silk, and with ceiling and doorways painted in delicate arabesque by Angelica Kauffmann, all combine to produce an extraordinary impression of culture and elegance and established power.

Yet, they are not palaces. There is something easygoing and unofficial about them. Between library and saloon one comes on little rooms, full of sporting prints and comfortable untidiness; the bedrooms upstairs are friendly with chintz and flowered wallpaper. Even the great rooms themselves, with their roomy writing tables, their armchairs, their tables piled with albums and commonplace books, seem designed less for state occasions than for private life: for leisure and lounging, for intimate talk, and desultory reading. And the portraits that glow down from the walls exhibit a similar character. The gentlemen lean back in their hunting coats, the ladies stroll in their parks with spaniels snapping at the ribbons that dangle from the garden hats, slung on their arms. In big and in detail these houses convey an effect of splendid naturalness. In this they are typical of the society which was their creator.

The Whig aristocracy was a unique product of English civilization. It was before all things a governing class. At a time when economic power was concentrated in the landed interest, the Whigs were among the biggest landowners: their party was in office for the greater part of the eighteenth century; during this period they possessed a large proportion of the seats in the House of

Commons; they produced more ambassadors and officers of state than the rest of England put together. And they lived on a scale appropriate to their power. "A man," said one of their latest representatives, "can jog along on £40,000 a year." And jog very well they did. They possessed, most of them, a mansion in London and two or three in the country; they moved through the world attended by a vast retinue of servants, of secretaries and chaplains, of companions, librarians and general hangers-on; they never travelled but in their own carriages; they kept open house to a continuous stream of guests, whom they entertained in the baroque and lavish style approved by their contemporaries.

For the elaboration of their life was increased by the period they lived in. The eighteenth century, that accomplished age, did not believe in the artless and the austere. In its view the good man or, as they would have phrased it, "the man of sense and taste," was he whose every activity was regulated in the light of a trained judgment and the experience of the wise in his own and former ages. From his earliest years the Whig nobleman was subjected to a careful education. He was grounded in the classics first by a tutor, then at Eton, then at the University. After this he went abroad for two years' grand tour to learn French and good manners in the best society of the continent. His sisters learnt

3

French and manners equally thoroughly at home; and their demeanour was further improved by a course of deportment. The Whigs' taste was in harmony with the ideal that guided their education. They learnt to admire the grand style in painting, the "correct" in letters, the Latin tradition in oratory. And in everything they paid strict attention to form. Since life to them was so secure and so pleasant, the Whig aristocrats tended to take its fundamental values very much for granted; they concentrated rather on how to live. And here again, their ideal was not an artless one. Their customs, their mode of speech, their taste in decoration, their stylish stiff clothes, are alike marked by a character at once polished and precise, disciplined and florid. If one of them writes a note it is rounded with a graceful phrase, their most extempore speeches are turned with a flourish of rotund rhetoric.

Yet—and here it is that it differs from those of similar societies on the continent—theirs was not an unreal life; no Watteau-like paradise of exquisite trifling and fastidious idleness. For one thing it had its roots in the earth. Founded as their position was on landed property, the Whig aristocracy was never urban. They passed at least half the year in their country seats; and there they occupied themselves in the ordinary avocations of country life. The ladies interested themselves in their children, and visited the poor; the gentlemen looked after their estates, rode to hounds, and administered from the local bench justice to poachers and pilferers. Their days went by, active out-of-door, unceremonious; they wore riding-boots as often as silk stockings. Moreover, they were always in touch with the central and serious current of contemporary life. The fact that they were a governing class meant that they had to govern. The Whig lord was as often as not a minister, his eldest son an M.P., his second attached to a foreign embassy. So that their houses were alive with the effort and hurry of politics. Red Foreign Office boxes strewed the library tables; at any time of day or night a courier might come galloping up with critical news, and the minister must post off to London to attend a Cabinet meeting. He had his work in the country too. He was a landlord and magistrate, often a lord lieutenant. While every few years would come a general election when his sons, if not himself, might have to sally forth to stand on the hustings and be pelted with eggs and dead cats by the free and independent electors of the neighbouring borough. Indeed his was not a protected existence. The eighteenth century was the age of clubs; and Whig society itself was a sort of club, exclusive, but in which those who managed to achieve membership lived on equal terms; a rowdy, rough-and-tumble club, full of conflict and plain speaking,

5

where people were expected to stand up for themselves and take and give hard knocks. At Eton the little dukes and earls cuffed and bullied each other like street urchins. As mature persons in their country homes, or in the pillared rooms of Brooks's Club, their intercourse continued more politely, yet with equal familiarity. While their House of Commons life passed in a robust atmosphere of combat and crisis and defeat. The Whigs despised the royal family; and there was certainly none of the hush and punctilio of court existence about them. Within the narrow limits of their world they were equalitarians.

Their life, in fact, was essentially a normal life, compounded of the same elements as those of general humanity, astir with the same clamour and clash and aspiration and competition as filled the streets round their august dwellings. Only, it was normal life played out on a colossal stage and with magnificent scenery and costumes. Their houses were homes, but homes with sixty bedrooms, set in grounds five miles round; they fought to keep their jobs, but the jobs were embassies and prime ministerships; their sons went to the same universities as humbler students, but were distinguished from them there by a nobleman's gold-tasselled mortarboard. When the Duke of Devonshire took up botany, he sent out a special expedition to the East Indies to search for rare plants; Lord Egremont liked pictures, so he filled a gallery with Claudes and Correggios; young Lord Palmerston was offered the Chancellorship of the Exchequer a year or two after entering Parliament.

This curiously-blended life produced a curiously blended type of character. With so many opportunities for action, its interests were predominantly active. Most of the men were engaged in politics. And the women— for they lived to please the men—were political too. They listened, they sympathized, they advised; through them two statesmen might make overtures to each other, or effect a reconciliation. But politics then were not the life sentence to hard labour that in our iron age they have become. Parliament only sat for a few months in the year; and even during the session, debates did not start till the late afternoon. The Whigs had the rest of their time to devote to other things. If they were sporting they raced and hunted; if interested in agriculture they farmed on an ambitious scale; if artistic they collected marbles and medals; if intellectual they read history and philosophy; if literary they composed compliments in verse and sonorous, platitudinous orations. But the chief of their spare time was given up to social life. They gave balls, they founded clubs, they played cards, they got up private theatricals: they cultivated friendship, and every variety, platonic and less platonic, of the art of love. Their ideal was the Renaissance ideal of the whole man, whose aspiration it is to make the most of every advantage, intellectual and sensual, that life has to offer.

In practice, of course, this ideal was not so broad as it sounds. The Whigs could not escape the limitations imposed by the splendour of their circumstances. Like all aristocrats they tended to be amateurs. When life is so free and so pleasant, a man is not likely to endure the drudgery necessary to make himself really expert in any one thing. Even in those affairs of state which took up most of the Whigs' time, they troubled little with the dry details of economic theory or administrative practice. Politics to them meant first of all personalities, and secondly general principles. And general principles to them were an occasion for expression rather than thought. They did not dream of questioning the fundamental canons of Whig orthodoxy. All believed in ordered liberty, low taxation and the enclosure of land; all disbelieved in despotism and democracy. Their only concern was to restate these indisputable truths in a fresh and effective fashion.

Again, their taste was a little philistine. Aristocratic taste nearly always is. Those whose ordinary course of life is splendid and satisfying, find it hard to recognize the deeper value of the exercises of the solitary imagination; art to them is not the fulfilment of the soul, but an ornamental appendage to existence. Moreover, the English nobility were too much occupied with practical affairs to achieve the fullest intellectual life. They admired what was elegant, sumptuous and easy to understand; portraits that were good likenesses and pleasing decorations; architecture which appropriately housed a stately life. In books, they appreciated acute, wittily phrased observation of human nature, or noble sentiments expressed in flowing periods; Cicero, Pope, Horace, Burke. The strange and the harsh they dismissed immediately. Among contemporary authors they appreciated Jane Austen, condemned Crabbe, for the most part, as sordid and low; and neglected Blake almost entirely. If they had read him, they would not have liked him. For—it is another of their limitations—they were not spiritual. Their education did not encourage them to be; and, anyway, they found this world too absorbing to concern themselves much with the next. The bolder spirits among them were atheists. The average person accepted Christianity, but in a straightforward spirit, innocent alike of mysticism and theological exactitude.

Further, their circumstances did not encourage the virtues of self-control. Good living gave them zest; wealth gave them opportunity; and they threw themselves into their pleasures with an animal recklessness at once terrifying and exhilarating to a modern reader. The most respectable people often drank themselves under the table without shocking anyone. "Colonel Napier came in to-night as drunk as an owl," remarks Lady Sarah Napier, of the staid middle-aged gentleman who was her husband. And their drinking was nothing to their gambling. Night after night they played loo and faro from early evening till the candles guttered pale in the light of the risen sun. Lord Stavordale lamented he had not been playing higher, on a night when he won £11,000 in a single hand at hazard. Georgiana, Duchess of Devonshire, cost her husband nearly £1,-000,000 in card debts. Rich as they were, they often ruined themselves. The letters of the time are loud with lamentations about the duns coming in and the furniture going out. Nor was their sexual life of a kind to commend them to an austere morality. "I was afraid I was going to have the gout the other day," writes Lord Carlisle to a friend, "I believe I live too chaste: it is not a common fault with me." It was not a common fault with any of them. In fact an unmarried man was thought unpleasantly queer, if he did not keep under his protec-,tion some sprightly full-bosomed Kitty Clive or Mrs. Bellamy, whose embraces he repaid with a house in Montpelier Square, a box at the opera, and a smart cabriolet in which to drive her down to Brighthelmstone for a week's amorous relaxation. Nor did he confine himself to professional ladies of pleasure. Even unmarried girls like Lady Hester Stanhope were suspected of having lovers; among married women the practice was too common to stir comment. The historian grows quite giddy as he tries to disentangle the complications of heredity consequent on the free and easy habits of the English aristocracy. The Harley family, children of the Countess of Oxford, were known as the Harleian Miscellany on account of the variety of fathers alleged to be responsible for their existence. The Duke of Devonshire had three children by the Duchess and two by Lady Elizabeth Foster, the Duchess one by Lord Grey; and most of them were brought up together in Devonshire House, each set of children with a surname of its own. "Emily, does it never strike you," writes Miss Pamela Fitzgerald in 1816, "the vices are wonderfully prolific among Whigs? There are such countless illegitimates, such a tribe of children of the mist." It is noteworthy that the author of this lively comment was a carefully brought up young lady of the highest breeding. The free habits of these days encouraged free speech. "Comfortable girls," remarks a middle-aged lady of her growing nieces, "who like a dirty joke." And the men, as can be imagined, were a great deal freer than the women. For all their polish the Whigs were not refined people in the Victorian sense of the word.

It appears in other aspects of their lives. They could be extremely arrogant; treating their inferiors with a patrician insolence which seems to us the reverse of good breeding. Lady Catherine de Bourgh was not the caricature that an ignorant person might suppose. Fashionable young men of refined upbringing amused themselves by watching fights where the Game Chicken battered the Tutbury Pet into unconsciousness with bare and blood-stained fists. And the pamphlets, the squibs, the appalling political cartoons that lay open in the most elegant drawing-rooms show that the ladies of the day were not squeamish either.

Still, unseemly as some of its manifestations were, one must admit that there is something extremely attractive in this earthy exuberance. And, as a matter of fact, it was the inevitable corollary of their virtues. English society had the merits of its defects. Its wide scope, its strong root in the earth, gave it an astounding, an irresistible vitality. For all their dissipation there was nothing decadent about these eighteenth century aristocrats. Their excesses came from too much life, not too little. And it was the same vitality that gave them their predominance in public life. They took on the task of directing England's destinies with the same self-confident vigour, that they drank and diced. It was this vigour that made Pitt Prime Minister at twenty-four years old,* that enabled the Foxites to keep the flag of liberty flying against the united public opinion of a panic-stricken nation. Nor did they let their pleasures interfere with these more serious activities. After eighteen hours of uninterrupted gambling, Charles Fox would arrive at the House of Commons to electrify his fellow members by a brilliant discourse on American taxation. Rakes and ladies of fashion intersperse their narratives of intrigue with discussions on politics, on literature, even on morals. For they were not unmoral. Their lapses came from passion not from principle; and they are liable at any time to break out in contrite acknowledgments of guilt, and artless resolutions for future improvement. Indeed it was one of the paradoxes created by their mixed composition that, though they were worldly, they were not sophisticated. Their elaborate manners masked simple reactions. Like their mode of life their characters were essentially natural; spontaneous, unintrospective, brimming over with normal feelings, love of home and family, loyalty, conviviality, desire for fame, hero-worship, patriotism. And they showed their feelings too. Happy

* Pitt diverged from the Whigs in later life: but he was brought up among them; and is, so far, representative of the Whig tradition.

creatures! They lived before the days of the stiff upper lip and the inhibited public school Englishman. A manly tear stood in their eye at the story of a heroic deed: they declared their loves in a strain of flowery hyperbole. They were the more expressive from their very unself-consciousness. It never struck them that they needed to be inarticulate to appear sincere. They were equally frank about their less elevated sentiments. Eighteenth century rationalism combined with rural common sense to make them robustly ready to face unedifying facts. And they declared their impressions with a brusque honesty, outstandingly characteristic of them. From Sir Robert Walpole who encouraged coarse conversation on the ground that it was the only form of talk which everyone enjoyed, down to the Duke of Wellington who described the army of his triumphs as composed of "the scum of the earth, enlisted for drink," the Augustan aristocracy, Whig and Tory alike, said what they thought with a superb disregard for public opinion. For if they were not original they were independent-minded. The conventions which bounded their lives were conventions of form only. Since they had been kings of their world from birth they were free from the tiresome inhibitions that are induced by a sense of inferiority. Within the locked garden of their society, individuality flowered riotous and rampant. Their typical figures show up beside the muted introverts of to-day as clear-cut and idiosyncratic as characters in Dickens. They took for granted that you spoke your mind and followed your impulses. If these were odd they were amused but not disapproving. They enjoyed eccentrics; George Selwyn who never missed an execution, Beau Brummel who took three hours to tie his cravat. The firm English soil in which they were rooted, the spacious freedom afforded by their place in the world, allowed personality to flourish in as many bold and fantastic shapes as it pleased.

But it was always a garden plant, a civilized growth. Whatever their eccentricities, the Whig nobles were never provincial and never uncouth. They had that effortless knowledge of the world that comes only to those, who from childhood have been accustomed to move in a complex society; that delightful unassertive confidence possible only to people who have never had cause to doubt their social position. And they carried to the finest degree of cultivation those social arts which engaged so much of their time. Here we come to their outstanding distinction. They were the most agreeable society England has ever known. The character of their agreeability was of a piece with the rest of them; mundane, straightforward, a trifle philistine, largely concerned with gossip, not given to subtle analyses or flights

15

of fancy. But it had all their vitality and all their sense of style. It was incomparably racy and spontaneous and accomplished; based solidly on a wide culture and experience, yet free to express itself in bursts of high spirits, in impulses of appreciation, in delicate movements of sentiment, in graceful compliments. For it had its grace; a virile classical grace like that of the Chippendale furniture which adorned its rooms, lending a glittering finish to its shrewd humour, its sharp-eyed observation, its vigorous disquisitions on men and things. Educated without pedantry, informal but not slipshod, polished but not precious, brilliant without fatigue, it combined in an easy perfection the charms of civilization and nature. Indeed the whole social life of the period shines down the perspective of history like some masterpiece of natural art; a prize bloom, nurtured in shelter and sunshine and the richest soil, the result of generations of breeding and blending, that spreads itself to the open sky in strength and beauty.

It was at its most characteristic in the middle of the century, it was at its most dazzling towards its close. By 1780 a new spirit was rising in the world. Ossian had taught people to admire ruins and ravines, Rousseau to examine the processes of the heart; with unpowdered heads and the ladies in simple muslin dresses, they paced the woods meditating, in Cowperlike mood, on the tender influences of nature. Though they kept the style and good sense of their fathers, their sympathies were wider. At the same time their feelings grew more refined. The hardness, which had marred the previous age, dwindled. Gainsborough, not Hogarth, mirrored the taste of the time; sensibility became a fashionable word. For a fleeting moment Whig society had a foot in two worlds and made the best of both of them. The lucid outline of eighteenth-century civilization was softened by the glow of the romantic dawn.

Dawn—but for them it was sunset. The same spirit that tinged them with their culminating glory was also an omen of their dissolution. For the days of aristocratic supremacy were numbered. By the iron laws which condition the social structure of man's existence, it could only last as long as it maintained an economic predominance. With the coming of the Industrial Revolution this predominance began to pass from the landlords to other ranks of the community. Already by the close of the century, go-ahead manufacturers in the north were talking of Parliamentary reform; already, in the upper rooms of obscure London alleys, working men met together to clamour for liberty, equality, and fraternity. Within forty years of its zenith, the Whig world was completely swept away. Only a few survivors lingered on to illustrate to an uncomprehending generation the charm of the past. Of these the most distinguished was William Lamb, second Viscount Melbourne.

PART I

Chapter I

THE LAMB
FAMILY

ODDLY enough, he did not come from an aristocratic family. By the stringent standards of the age the Lambs were parvenus. Their fortunes had been founded three generations before, by Peniston Lamb, an attorney of humble origin in Nottinghamshire, who died leaving a fortune of £100,000. His heir, a nephew called Matthew, was even more successful. With the help of his legacy he married an heiress, bought a country place, entered the House of Commons, and eventually acquired a baronetcy. Here the family progress seemed likely to stop: his son, Sir Peniston Lamb, was a less effective personality. He makes his first appearance on the stage of history as a young man of fashion writing to his mistress, the notorious Mrs. Sophia Baddeley. "I send you a million kissis, remember I love you Satterday, Sunday, every day . . . I hope you will get the horsis, but I beg you will not be so ventersum, as there are bad horsis, but will get one quite quiett . . . pray destroy all letters lest anyone should find them by axcedent." Mrs. Baddeley found the author of these artless communications child's play. She deceived him often and flagrantly; but he always believed her protestations of innocence, and seldom visited her without bringing a £200 bill in his pocket as a present. Indeed his only noticeable characteristic seems to have been a capacity for getting rid of money. Handsome, festive and foolish, his main occupation was to squander the guineas laboriously accumulated for him by his forefathers. His money raised him to the peerage of Ireland as first Baron Melbourne, and procured him a seat in Parliament. But during the forty years he spent there, he only opened his mouth once. Such energy as he possessed was fully employed in drinking port, following the hounds, and playing faro at Almack's Club.

However, any deficiencies on his part were more than made up for by his wife. Elizabeth Milbanke, Lady Melbourne was one of the most remarkable women of her age. Not that she was original. On the contrary, she was a typical eighteenth-century woman of the world:

ELIZABETH MILBANKE Viscountess Melbourne in youth
*From a painting by Thomas Phillips in the possession
of the Lord Leconfield*

but with all the qualities of her type intensified to the highest degree. She was very beautiful in the style approved by her contemporaries; "a fine woman," with a clear-cut mouth, challenging dark eyes, and a figure moulded in the shapely contours which stirred the full-blooded desires of the gentlemen of Brooks's Club. Nor did they find her a disappointment on closer acquaintance. Her temperament was as full-blooded as their own; and she was even more satisfactory as a companion than she was as a lover. It was not exactly that she had charm: there was nothing appealing about her, nothing intoxicating, nothing mysterious. The cool, astringent atmosphere exhaled by her personality suggested prose rather than poetry. But it was singularly agreeable prose, at once soothing and stimulating. She could be amusing in a direct, caustic way; and she understood the art of getting on with men completely. Level-tempered and rational, she found scenes and caprices as tiresome as they did. After the unaccountable moods of stormier sirens, it was infinitely delightful to find oneself "laughing away an hour" on the sofa of her sitting-room in Melbourne House, with Lady Melbourne—Lady Melbourne, who could be depended upon never to be touchy, or exacting, or shocked, or low-spirited, who did not expect men to be monogamous, and who never asked an awkward question. She seemed to combine the social merits of both

23

sexes, to possess, at the same time, male robustness and feminine tact, a woman's voluptuousness and a man's judgment. Moreover, she had an unusual power of entering into a man's interests. She disliked talking about herself; "no man is safe with another's secrets, no woman with her own," she once remarked. But she threw herself whole-heartedly into other people's problems; was always ready to listen sympathetically to a man's complaints about wives and political leaders, to advise him about how to manage a mistress, or an estate agent. And excellent advice it was too: Lady Melbourne's masculine point of view was the product of a masculine intelligence. By choice it showed itself in practical affairs; her friends noted with irritation that she was the only woman who made her garden a paying concern. But if she did turn her attention to other matters—to politics, for instance —her opinion was always shrewd and judicious. In a positive, plain-sailing way she was a very able woman. And, within the limits of her experience, she had an uncommon knowledge of life. No one had a clearer understanding of the social machine, no one could give a man a more accurate idea of the forces to be reckoned with in planning a career; no one could tell one better how to satisfy one's desires without offending convention. Deliberately to defy it was, in her eyes, as silly as deliberately to defy the law of gravity. "Anyone who braves the opinion of the world," she used to say, "sooner or later feels the consequences of it."

Her character was in keeping with the rest of her. She had the virtues of her common sense and her full-bloodedness. Though pleasure-loving she was not shallow. Her vigour of spirit showed itself also in her feelings. She cared for few people; but these she loved with a strong, unegotistic affection that could be absolutely depended upon. No effort was too great that might advance their interests. Yet, her feelings were always controlled by her judgment. In the most vertiginous complications of intrigue and dissipation, Lady Melbourne could be relied on to remain dignified and collected. And reasonable; her philosophy taught her that the world must be kept going. And to ensure its smooth working she was always prepared to make sacrifices. She had strong dislikes, but could suppress them in the cause of common peace: even though a woman might have lovers, it was no excuse, in her view, for her neglecting her duty to her family, or acting in such a way as to outrage social standards.

All the same it is impossible to approve of Lady Melbourne. Her outlook was both low and limited. To her the great world of rank and fashion was the only world; and she saw it as a battle ground in which most people fought for their own ends. Nor was hers an amiable cynicism. She was good-tempered, not good-natured;

suave, but not soft. Her laughter was satirical and un-
feeling, she could not resist a wounding thrust. And,
on the rare occasions she judged it wise to lose her temper,
she was both relentless and brutal. Indeed, in spite of
her polish, there was something essentially coarse-fibred
about her. She cared little what others did so long as
they kept up appearances. And herself, if she found it
convenient, would plot and make use of people without
compunction.

But all her qualities, good and bad, were subordinated
to one presiding motive, ambition. Since to her this world
was the only one, its prizes seemed to her the only objects
worth having. And her whole life was given up to getting them for herself and for her family. To this end she
dedicated her beauty, her brains and her energy: it was
for this she learned to be sagacious and smiling, tactful
and dignified, ruthless and cunning. A single purpose
united every element in her personality. Here we come to
the secret of her eminence. It was not that she was more
gifted than many of her rivals, but that her gifts were
more concentrated. Amid a humanity frustrated by conflicting aspirations and divided desires, Lady Melbourne
stood out all of a piece; her character, her talents, moved
steadily and together, towards the same goal. One might
suspect her, but one could not withstand her will. And
so smoothly did life move under her sway, her judgment

evinced so rational a grasp of reality, that in the end she generally brought one round to her view.

From the first she was successful. Her birth was higher than her husband's; Sir Ralph Milbanke, her father, was the head of an old Yorkshire county family. But it was early clear that his daughter was marked for a more brilliant destiny than could be achieved in provincial Yorkshire. Before she was seventeen she had married Lord Melbourne and his fortune, had established herself in his splendid family mansion in Piccadilly—it occupied the site where the Albany stands now—had re-decorated it in white and gold, and had begun her seige of London. Her chief weapon, naturally enough, was her power over men. She could not, indeed, make much of Lord Melbourne. "I am tired to death," he writes to Mrs. Baddeley, "with prancing about with my Betsy a-shopping." And shopping was about all he was good for. When he had bought her some diamonds and paid for the gold paint, he had done all that a reasonable woman could expect of him. However there were other men in the world; and Lady Melbourne lost no time in making their acquaintance. Characteristically she contrived that those she selected for peculiar favours should be both agreeable and useful. During the course of her career her name was to be coupled with the fashionable Lord Coleraine and the powerful Duke of Bedford. But the most im-

portant man in her life was Lord Egremont. He was a
worthy counterpart to her. Except that he did not care
for politics, George Wyndham, third Earl of Egremont,
was the pattern grand seigneur of his time. At once distinguished and unceremonious, rustic and scholarly, he
spent most of his time at his palace of Petworth in a life
of magnificent hedonism, breeding horses, collecting
works of art, and keeping open house for a crowd of
friends and dependants. He had the eccentricities of his
type. Too restless to remain in any one place for more
than five minutes, he would suddenly appear in the room
where his guests were sitting, smiling benevolently and
with his hat on; would make a few genial remarks often
revealing considerable erudition, and then go away; an
hour or two later he would reappear, continue the conversation just where he had left it off, and after another
few minutes, vanish again. He had a number of children
by various mistresses; but did not marry until late in
life, owing to the influence of Lady Melbourne. How
their connection arose is not known. Scandal had it that
he bought her from Lord Coleraine for £13,000, of which
she took a share. It is an unlikely story; he was attractive
enough to win her on his own merits and she seems to
have been genuinely devoted to him. All we know for
certain is that by 1779 Lord Egremont was established as
her most trusted adviser and chief lover. What Lord

Melbourne thought of his Betsy's amorous activities is also obscure. People noticed that he did not seem to like his wife's friends. But he was not the man to make an effective protest; moreover, Lady Melbourne always took particular care never to put him in an awkward position.

However, she did not look exclusively to men for her advancement. It is the measure of her perspicacity that she realized that the security of a woman's social position depends on the support given her by her own sex. And she set her wits to get it. So successfully, that within a few years of coming to London she had become a close friend of the most famous fashionable leader of the day, the ravishing Duchess of Devonshire. It was an unnatural intimacy. For one thing Lady Melbourne was essentially a man's woman; it was only with men that she felt sufficiently sure of her ground to be her robust self; with women she was at best no more than smooth and pleasant. Further, the Duchess was her opposite in every respect, refined, imprudent and emotional. But affinity of the spirit is not so necessary for friendship in the rush of fashionable life, as in soberer circles. It is enough to be agreeable and to enjoy the same pleasures. Lady Melbourne passed both these tests easily: besides, her discretion combined with her interest in other people's doings to make her the perfect confidante of the poor Duchess's tangled romances. When the outraged Duke banished her for some months to France, it was Lady Melbourne whom she chose to keep her in touch with her disconsolate lover, Mr. Grey.

What with the Duchess and Lord Egremont, Lady Melbourne's path was now easy. From the records of the day we catch glimpses of her during her dazzling progress; driving surrounded by gentlemen on horseback amid the shelving glades of her country home at Brocket; piquant in the costume of a macaroni at a masquerade at the Pantheon; adjusting her feathers before the glass while she discusses stocks and shares with Horace Walpole; dancing, "to his great delight, though in rather a cowlike style," with the Prince of Wales. For in 1784 she made her most distinguished conquest; she captured the affections of the future George IV. It was not for long— it never was with him. But Lady Melbourne saw to it that, even when all was over, they remained firm friends. In the meantime she took the opportunity to get Lord Melbourne made a Lord of the Bedchamber. Already in 1781 he had, by her efforts, been raised to a Viscounty. Even in the flush of her triumphs, she never forgot to use them for the acquisition of more lasting benefits. By 1785 she was securely fixed in that social position for which she had worked so hard.

It was not, it was never going to be, the best sort of social position. There was always a section of the beau

THE LAMB FAMILY

monde who looked askance at Lady Melbourne as an
upstart, and a shady upstart at that. Gentlemen still joked
about Lord Coleraine and his £13,000; rival beauties alleged that Lady Melbourne could not see a happy marriage without wanting to break it up. But eighteenth
century society accepted people, whatever their sins, as
long as they kept its rules of decorum. Lady Melbourne
was an expert at these rules. Audacious but completely
in control, she knew just how close she could sail to the
wind without disaster. And if she was not the most re-
spected woman in society, she was among the very
smartest. Melbourne House was recognized as one of the
liveliest social centres in London. Day after day the great
doors opened and shut to admit the cleverest men and
the most fascinating women in the town; untidy delightful Fox; Sheridan sparkling and a little drunk; the dark
Adonis of diplomacy, Lord Granville Leveson-Gower; the
Duchess of Devonshire and her sister Lady Bessborough,
the witty Mr. Hare, the artistic Mrs. Damer. While every
few weeks at one in the morning the tables were spread
and the candles lit for a supper party to the Prince of
Wales.

Nor was Melbourne House merely a modish meeting-
place. Social life there was a creation, with its own
particular charm, its own particular flavour. It was the
flavour of its mistress's personality; virile, easy-going,

31

astringent. Manners were casual; elaborate banquets, huge rooms frescoed by Bartolozzi went along with un-punctualness and informality. "That great ocean," says the orderly Lady Granville in a moment of exasperation, "where a person is forced to shift for himself without clue; they wander about all day and sleep about all the evening; no meal is at a given hour, but drops upon them as an unexpected pleasure." And the mental atmosphere, too, was not fastidious. The spirit of Melbourne House offered no welcome to the new romanticism. It was plain-spoken, it laughed uproariously at fancifulness and fine feelings, it enjoyed bold opinions calculated to shock the prudish and the over-sensitive, it loved derisively to strip a character of its ideal pretensions. From mischief though, rather than from bitterness; an unflagging good humour was one of its two distinguishing attractions. The other was its intellectual vigour. The inhabitants of Melbourne House were always ready for an argument; about Whig policy or the character of the Royal family or Miss Burney's new novel or Mr. Godwin's curious theories; shrewd, hard-hitting arguments full of assertion and contradiction, but kept light by the flash of wit and the accomplishment of men of the world.

The creator of such a circle might well feel justified in sitting back to rest on her laurels. Not so Lady Melbourne; her vitality only matured with years. Though

a little fatter than she had been, she was still able to attract men and still willing to do so. But she was far too
sensible to let herself lapse into the deplorable role of a
fading siren. From the age of thirty-five or so the energy
of her ambition centred itself on her children. In this,
it followed natural inclination. The instincts of her normal dominating nature made her strongly maternal; it
was on her children that she expended the major force
of her narrow and powerful affections. Lord Melbourne
took the same secondary part in their lives as he did elsewhere. As a matter of fact he was only doubtfully related
to them. They were six in number: Peniston, born 1770,
William, born 1779, Frederic, born 1782, George, born
1784, Emily, born 1787, and another daughter, Harriet,
who died before she grew up. Of these, William was universally supposed to be Lord Egremont's son, George, the
Prince of Wales', while Emily's birth was shrouded in
mystery. Nor had Lord Melbourne the character to
achieve by force of personality that authority with which
he had not been endowed by nature. On two occasions
only is he recorded to have expressed his will with regard
to his children. He rebuked William when he first grew
up for following the new-fangled fashion of short hair:
and he was very much annoyed with Harriette Wilson for
refusing to become Frederic's mistress. "Not have my
son, indeed," he said, "six foot high and a fine strong

33

handsome able young fellow. I wonder what she would have." And meeting Miss Wilson, taking a morning walk on the Steyne at Brighton, he told her what he thought of her.* Such efforts were not of a kind to win him any exaggerated respect from his children. They regarded him with kindly contempt, varied by moments of irritation. "Although Papa only drinks a glass of negus," writes his daughter Emily some years later, "somehow or other he contrives to be *drunkish,*" and again, "by some fatality Papa is always wrong and I pass my life in trying to set him right."

They viewed Lady Melbourne with different feelings. Indeed, she was a better mother than many more estimable persons. To the task of her children's education she brought all her intelligence and all her knowledge of life. In the first place she saw to it that they had a good time. For the most part they lived at Brocket— Brocket, that perfect example of the smaller country house of the period, with its rosy, grey-pilastered façade, its urbane sunny sitting rooms, its charming park like a landscape by Wilson, where, backed by woods, the turf sweeps down to a stream spanned by a graceful bridge of cut stone. Here the little Lambs played, and rode, and had reading lessons from their Jersey bonne. They

---

* This, like all Harriette Wilson's stories, must be taken as only doubtfully authoritative.

were to be met at Melbourne House, too, running round
the courtyard, or off to Sir Joshua Reynolds' or Mr. Hoppner's studio to sit for their portraits. And all round
them, now loud, now muffled by nursery doors, but so
continuous that it seemed like the rumour of life itself,
sounded ever the huge confused hum of the great world.
Often they caught an actual glimpse of it. Playing on the
stairs, a child's eye would be arrested by the shapely
silken legs of the Prince of Wales as he walked, "fit to
leap out of his skin" with spirits, from Lady Melbourne's
sitting room. "Have you had your dinner yet?" he would
ask, for he was fond of children and took notice of them.
Sometimes they would be taken down for a visit to Petworth to gaze on the troops of Arab horses and the queer
looking people, artists and antiquaries, with which Lord
Egremont filled his house. Time passed; the elder boys
went to school, first with a clergyman near Brocket, and
then at nine years old to Eton, each of them with ten
guineas in his pocket, and five shillings a week more to
be supplied by a servant at the local inn. Eton was an
easy-going place then: unhampered by the virtuous discipline of organized games, the boys spent their leisure
rabbit-snaring, attending dog fights, stuffing at the pastry
cooks when they were small, and getting tipsy on beer
when they were bigger; while after Peniston had left
he would come down and take one of his brothers over

to Ascot for a week's racing. In between whiles came holidays; riding and shooting and theatricals, and now and again a visit to the professional playhouse. It was a very pleasant life. But Lady Melbourne did more than just amuse her children. In the most hectic whirl of her social engagements, she found time to exert a persistent and purposeful influence on them. Her great carriage was always carrying her down to Eton: where, with characteristic efficiency, she combined her visit with a dinner to the Prince of Wales, if he happened to be at Windsor. Sedulously she studied her children's characters, promoted their tastes, encouraged their ambitions. She read with them, wrote to them, she talked things over with them with a light and artful frankness that kept them always at their ease. Her diligence met with its reward. They had a profound respect for her judgment, and they were devoted to her. Further, they were devoted to each other. By the time they were grown up Lady Melbourne had contrived to weld them together into that strongest of social units, a compact family group; with its own standards, its own idiom of thought and speech, its own jokes; confronting the world with the cheerful confidence that, where it differed from others, it was right and the others were wrong.

This corporate personality was the appropriate product of its parentage and environment. Strikingly handsome, with their tall, well-made figures, firmly-cut countenances and dark eyes brilliant with animation, the Lambs were alike vital, sensual, clever, positive, and unidealistic. People did not always take to them. They complained that they were hard and mocking, unappreciative of delicacy and romance; they were scandalized by the freedom alike of their morals and their conversation; and they disliked their manners. The boys, especially, ate greedily and were liable suddenly to go to sleep and snore; they asserted their opinions with arrogance, interlarded their speech with oaths, and laughed very loud. Yet they attracted more than they repelled. It was difficult to dislike people with such splendid talent for living. Love, sport, wine, food, they entered with zest into every pleasure. And their minds were equally responsive; alert to note and assess character and event with quick perspicacity. Born and bred citizens of the world, they knew their way about it by a sort of infallible instinct. And they had an instinctive mastery of its social arts. Their negligence was never boorish; it arose from the fact that they felt so much at home in life that they were careless of its conventions. Superficial brusqueness masked an unfailing adroitness in the management of situations: their talk was as dexterous as it was unaffected; its bluntness was made delightful by their peculiar brand of jovial incisive humour. For they possessed—it was their chief charm

37

—in the highest degree, the high spirits of their home. A lazy sunshine of good humour shone round them, softening the edge of their sharpest sayings. Though they thought poorly of the world, they enjoyed every moment of it: not to do so seemed to them the last confession of failure. "What stuff people are made of," said one of them, "who find life and society tiresome when they are in good health and have neither liver nor spleen affected; and have spirits enough to enjoy, instead of being vexed by, the ordinary little tracasseries of life." This sentence might have stood for the family motto.

Within the frame of this common character, individual differences revealed themselves. Beautiful Peniston, the eldest, was the only one with a touch of Lord Melbourne: he had brains but used them mainly on the turf. Frederic, on the other hand, was a finished man of the world; combining lively intellectual interests and a life of many loves by means of a tact that was later to make him a distinguished diplomat. Did he not read Shakespeare to his mistress: and, what was more, persuade her to enjoy it? George's character, riotous, hasty-tempered, and a trifle vulgar, gave colour to the report that he was the son of the Prince of Wales. An excellent comedian, he spent his spare time scribbling farces, and hobnobbing with the actors in the green-room of Drury Lane. Emily was a milder edition of her mother, with the same social gifts, the same amorous propensities; but softer, more easy-going, not so clever. The second son, William, was less typical.

He did not appear so on first acquaintance. With his manly, black-browed handsomeness, his scornful smile, his lounging manners, his careless perfection of dress—"no one," it was said, "ever *happened* to have coats that fitted better"—he looked the Lamb spirit incarnate. No less than his brothers he was genial and sensible, guzzled, swore and went to sleep, in argument he was the most arrogantly assertive of the lot. Yet, talking to him for any length of time, one became aware of a strain that did not harmonize with the Lamb atmosphere. When a subject arose peculiarly interesting to him, suddenly his smile would give place to an expression of ardent excitement; a pathetic tale brought the tears starting to his eyes; at other moments he would lapse unaccountably into a musing melancholy: then in a twinkling his old smiling nonchalance would reappear, as surprisingly as it had vanished. Indeed—it was to be the dominating factor in his subsequent history—there was a discord in the fundamental elements of his composition. Much of him was pure Lamb or rather pure Milbanke. He had the family zest for life, their common sense, their animal temperament. But some chance of heredity—it may well have been Egremont blood—had infused into this another strain, finer, and more unaccountable. His mind showed it. It was not just that he was cleverer than his brothers and sisters: but his intelligence worked on different lines, imaginative, disinterested, questioning. It enjoyed thought for its own sake, it was given to curious speculations, that had no reference to practical results. He could absorb himself in points of pure scholarship, sit up for hours studying history and poetry. Along with this cast of mind went a vein of acute sensibility. Affection was necessary to him, he loathed to give pain, he responded with swift sympathy to the appeal of the noble and the delicate. At his first school, he would sit gazing out of the window at the labourers at work in the placid Hertfordshire land-scape, and long to be one of them. And though this came no doubt mainly from a normal dislike of lessons, it was in keeping with an inborn appreciation of the charm of innocence and the pleasures of contemplation. Across the substantial, clear-coloured fabric of the man of the world were discernible incongruous streaks of the philoso-pher and the romantic.

So strangely-blended a disposition portended a complex and dissonant character. At odds with himself, he was bound also to be at odds with any world with which he came into contact. Certainly there was a great deal in him out of harmony with the earthy spirit of Melbourne House. Obscurely conscious of this perhaps, he was as a little boy stormier and more self-willed than his brothers and sister. However, very soon any such outward signs of conflict passed away. The growing William appeared unconcerned by the discrepancy between his nature and his environment—if, indeed, he was aware that it existed. His very desire to please made him adaptable. And circumstances encouraged his adaptability. Children brought up in gay and patrician surroundings seldom react against them with the violence common in more circumscribed lives. If their tastes differ from those of the people round them, they have the leisure and money to follow them up in some degree: and anyway their ordinary mode of living is too agreeable for them to conceive any strong aversion to it. Further, the Milbanke half of William's nature was perfectly suited by his home. He loved the parties and the sport and the gossip, he felt at home in the great world. Nor was his other side starved at Melbourne House. He had all the books he liked, he could listen enthralled to the clever men cleverly disputing. While his native tenderness bloomed in the steady sunshine of the family affection. His brothers and sister were as fond of him as of each other. And, in the half-laughing, unsentimental way approved by Lamb standards, they showed their feelings. He returned them. His brothers were always his closest men friends, his favourite boon companions. What could be better fun than acting with George, arguing with Frederic, racing with Peniston. He was equally attached to his sisters, especially "that little devil, Emily." Like many persons of a philosophical turn, he enjoyed giving instruction; would spend hours of his holidays superintending his sisters' pleasures, hearing them their lessons: when they were at Brocket and he in London, he wrote them long letters about the plays he had seen. But as might have been expected, his most important relationship was with his mother. He was the type of character that is always most susceptible to feminine influence. Men were excellent companions for a riotous evening or a rational talk. But it was only with women that he could get that intensely personal contact, that concentrated and intimate sympathy, of which his sensibility was in need. As a matter of fact, Lady Melbourne would have attracted him apart from her femininity. Her realism roused an answering chord in his own, her single-minded certainty was reassuring to his divided spirit. He pleased her as much as she pleased him. Was he not like Lord Egremont? Besides, her practised eye soon discerned that he was the cleverest of her children; and therefore the one most likely to realize her ambitions. William's happiness, William's success, became the chief interest of her later life. To mould his character and win his heart, she brought out every tested and glittering weapon in her armoury. She studied his disposition,

WILLIAM LAMB at seventeen in Montem Dress
From a painting by John Hoppner at Windsor Castle
(by gracious permission of H.M. The King)

fostered his talents, applauded his triumphs, kept up with his interests: read books with him; with him discussed the characters of his friends—all in the free-and-easy terms, the amused unshockable tone she employed with her mature men friends. This sometimes led to awkward consequences. Once when he was ten, he told her of a school fellow called Irby, the son of a family acquaintance. "Every Irby is a fool," remarked Lady Melbourne trenchantly. William thought it very true of this particular Irby: when he went back to Eton he told him so. He in his turn repeated it to his family; and a row ensued which must have needed all Lady Melbourne's celebrated tact to smooth over. But the incident had taught William his first lesson in discretion. And he never forgot it. Under her purposeful hands his character began to take form; a form in which his Milbanke side was uppermost. By twelve years old he was already equable, controlled, and possessed of a precocious capacity for adjusting himself to facts. His stormy temper was suppressed; as for any deeper sources of discontent with his environment, life was too full and amusing to worry about them.

In these circumstances it is not surprising that his childhood was happy. He loved Brocket; he did not mind his first school, though he preferred it when his parents were in London and he was not tantalized by the thought of the pleasures of home only a few miles away: Eton he enjoyed enormously. It was a little unnerving at first for one who, up till then, had not moved a step unattended by nurses or tutors, to find himself at nine years old alone in a crowd of seven hundred boys, all rampaging in the uproarious barbarity of the unreformed public school. But William was himself sufficiently uproarious soon to feel at home there: while his perspicacity, improved by Lady Melbourne's training, showed him how to adapt himself to school life in such a way as to suffer as little as possible from its inevitable drawbacks. He managed never to become a regular fag, and to be flogged very seldom. If he was, he did not repine, but forgot it as quickly as he could. The bloody duels of fisticuffs which were at that time the approved method of settling school-boy quarrels, presented a greater problem. William did not like fighting. However, here too, he found a way to make it as little disagreeable as possible. Soon after he went to Eton he had to fight a boy bigger than himself. "He pummelled me amazingly," he related, "and I saw I should never beat him; I stood and reflected a little and *thought* to myself and then gave it up. I thought it one of the most prudent acts, but it was reckoned very dastardly." However he remained blandly impervious to criticism so obviously inconsistent with common sense: from this time forward, he made it his sensible rule never to fight with anyone likely to beat him. "After the first

44

round if I found I could not lick the fellow, I said, 'come this won't do, I will go away; it is no use standing here to be knocked to pieces.' " So early did he evince that capacity for compromising genially with circumstances, which was to distinguish his later career.

For the rest he enjoyed everything; the drinking, the rabbit hunting, the jam tarts, the weeks with Peniston at Ascot, the Festival of Montem, when, gaudy in cavalier plumes and Hussar uniforms, the boys stood about in the streets dunning distinguished visitors for guineas. Naturally gregarious, he also got pleasure out of his school fellows. They were sometimes a little ridiculous: Brummell, for instance, with his drawling speech and dandified appearance, especially preposterous to William whose locks were always in a tangle. But ridiculous people added to the amusement of life; besides Brummell was an entertaining fellow, if you set yourself to get the best out of him. Nor was school life without more glorious sources of satisfaction. William did not work hard, at least after his first two years; but early grounding and a natural gift for scholarship kept him in a high place. By the time he left, he was one of the acknowledged kings of the school. Even the holidays seemed a little flat, back at Brocket with no fag to run clattering at his call, no clusters of sycophants to gaze admiringly at him and his co-monarchs as, in careless lordliness, they strolled the

Eton streets. There was no doubt that Eton, indolent, high-spirited, undisciplined Eton, was the school for him. During the rest of his life it was to linger in his memory, tinged with a golden sentiment; so that, forty years later, as a grey-headed statesman disillusioned by a lifetime of glory and agitation, he could never hear a clock like the Eton clock without a lift of happiness at his heart.

Chapter II

THE BEAU
MONDE

FOR CAMBRIDGE, where he went at seventeen, he could never feel the same affection. He was even less industrious there than at Eton. Rich young men always find it hard to work at a university, especially if they have the Lamb gift for pleasure. It is only the poor-spirited or the morbidly conscientious, who can go on doing lessons, in the flush of their first appearance in the world as mature young men, able to do whatever they please. William did not even trouble to follow the regular course; along with the rest of the gilded youth at Cambridge he spent the next four years revelling, talking and making friends; sauntering the streets by day, and sitting up over the port at night. However, he was

47

too active-minded to live without any intellectual occupation. He read a good deal in a desultory kind of way.
And it is likely that he profited more by so doing than
if he had kept himself to the narrow path of academic
study. His strong young brain, rejoicing in its own activity, ranged over an enormous variety of subjects. Mathe-
matics, indeed, he never cared for. They were too in-
human a science. But he read widely in the classics,
ancient and modern, he devoured history books, he delved
into the mysterious problems of ethical philosophy.
With this intellectual development came a growing interest in public affairs. His realism had not yet learnt
to apply itself to subjects outside his own experience; like
other clever young men he was attracted to the idealistic,
the daring, and the impractical; sentiments that roused
a glow in the generous breast; opinions calculated to send
a shiver down the spine of the timid and the conventional.
His hero was Fox, his party the extreme Whigs. With a
gloomy satisfaction he prophesied the ruin of his country
under the sway of the contemptible Tories. "We have
been for a long time the first nation in Europe," he remarked to his mother. "We have now lost our sovereignty and shall shortly be the last." As far as he could
see the best thing for England would be to be defeated
by the French under the enlightened Buonaparte. How
dreadful it was to think that our arms might drive him

48

out of Egypt. "I was in despair at hearing of the intentions of the French to evacuate Egypt. I was in hopes they would have been able to maintain themselves there in spite of Canning's wit and Sir Sidney's valour." Canning, now at the height of his polemical brilliance, was castigating his opponents in the Anti-Jacobin. But William could not think much of his intelligence. He supported the Tories, he must be a fool.

The more theoretical aspect of William's political ideas found expression in an oration he composed in competition for the university declamation prize. The subject was the progressive improvement of mankind. William treated it in a lofty vein. "Crime is a curse," so runs his peroration, "only to the period in which it is successful; but virtue, whether fortunate or otherwise, blesses not only its own age but remotest posterity." These edifying reflections met with a most gratifying reception. Not only did William win the prize, but the great Fox himself selected the passage in question to quote in the House of Commons. Nor was this William's only public success. He wrote poetry as well as reading it; translations from the classics, and occasional verses, in the orthodox Augustan manner, full of classical allusions and noble commonplaces. In 1798 he blossomed forth in print as a satirist, crossing swords with Canning in a reply to some verses in the Anti-Jacobin. His poem was passed round the clubs and drawing-rooms of the Metropolis, to the general approbation. It was not very good. But, then as now, London society was disposed to look kindly on the literary efforts of handsome young men of good family.

In addition to applauding his writing, they asked him out to dinner. His intellectual debut coincided with his social: in the vacations he made his first entry into the beau monde as a grown-up man. No one could have done it in more advantageous circumstances. Born in the centre of its most entertaining circle, he found himself, without any effort on his part, elected to its best clubs, invited to its most brilliant parties. And he had the talents to make the most of his advantages. It was true that he did not always make a good first impression. He had some of the conceit of his time of life, and more of its shyness. Even Lady Melbourne's training had not been able to free him from that self-consciousness which afflicts clever young men at nineteen years old: the thought of making a fool of himself in public haunted him. To escape it, he assumed an exaggeration of the family manner, adopted a contemptuous pose, as of one who disdained to compete in a world which he despised. Introduced to someone with whom he felt himself likely to be out of sympathy, an Anti-Jacobin, for instance, he turned away; now and again he would try and overcome

his nervousness by asserting, unnecessarily loudly, some
outrageous paradox. But all this was superficial. A few
minutes talk revealed that he was in reality unassuming,
appreciative, and as agreeable as Lady Melbourne herself.
Within a short time he was one of the most fashionable
young men in London.

Indeed, Whig society was his spiritual home; its order
of life, at once leisurely and lively, suited him down to
the ground. He rose late in the morning, breakfasted
largely, strolled up St. James's Street, to loiter for an
hour or two in the window of his Club, hearing the news,
surveying the world. Later might come a ride in the
park or an afternoon call; the evening was the time for
dinner parties followed by the opera, the theatre, or a
ball; then back to the Club for some supper till four or
five o'clock struck, and it was time to go to bed. William enjoyed it all. Music and dancing in themselves
did not please him; they were not the fashion among
smart young men of the day. But he was happy at any
sort of social gathering. And dinner parties he found
perfectly delightful: succulent sumptuous feasts twelve
courses long, then the pleasant hour with the gentlemen
over the wine, whence they emerged to join the ladies
about midnight. Several of the men, he noticed, were always drunk; but this did not displease him. "It tended
to increase the gaiety of society," he said, "it produced

diversity." After the session came the social life of the country; week long visits to Petworth or Bowood, where the mornings were spent reading, while the ladies sketched or played the harp; followed by sporting afternoons, and evenings when, after another enormous meal, the party sat up till three in the morning, playing cards, writing verses, organizing theatricals. The theatricals were a trial to William's self-consciousness. At Inverary he consented to take the part of Leander in a farce, but could not bring himself to appear publicly in the wreath of roses and bunches of cherry-coloured ribbon which the producer thought the correct costume for his role. Into the other amusements he entered with unalloyed enthusiasm. We find him editing a comic paper during a visit, contributing stanzas to Brummell's album; and he was ready to talk to anyone. With such accomplishments to recommend him he soon got on friendly terms with the most agreeable conversationalists of the day; Fox, Sheridan, Canning—whom he found very pleasant on closer acquaintance—Rogers, Monk Lewis, Tom Moore.

Mainly his social life centred round four houses, Carlton House, Holland House, Devonshire House and his own home. It was not the Piccadilly home of his childhood. In 1789 the Duke of York had taken a fancy to that: and Lady Melbourne, always ready to oblige influential persons, had agreed to exchange it for the Duke's own residence in Whitehall, that grey spreading pile of rusticated stone which is now the Scottish Office. However, re-decorated by its new mistress, the second Melbourne House was just as splendid as the first; and life there was equally brilliant, disorderly, and in the thick of things. Daily the gentlemen dropped in on their way to and from the House of Commons; nightly the courtyard re-echoed with the coach wheels that brought to dinner the Duchess of Devonshire, or the Prince of Wales. For a year or two there had been a coldness between the Prince and the Melbournes. He expected his friends to take his part in every chop and change of his endless quarrels. And when, after Mrs. Fitzherbert fell from favour, he discovered that Lady Melbourne continued to visit her, he broke with her entirely. But now in 1798 Mrs. Fitzherbert was forgiven and the Prince back at Melbourne House, in wilder spirits than ever, and eating on a scale which even William, accustomed though he was to the appetites of the day, found amazing. The Prince took a fancy to him, that was why William went so much to Carlton House. Few weeks passed that he did not walk across the Mall to dine within its meretricious walls; where he sat, an observant young man, listening to his royal host as, hour by hour, he poured forth the kaleidoscopic effusions of his preposterous egotism; now abusing his parents, now bragging of his amorous conquests, now courting the applause of the company by his vivid mimicry of Mr. Pitt or Lord North, now soliciting their sympathy by sentimental laments on the unexampled misery of his lot. It was very entertaining; it was also instructive. At Carlton House William got his first lesson in an art that was to be the instrument of his greatest success in later life, the art of getting on with royal personages. Lady Melbourne carried this instruction a step farther; she showed him how to manage them for their good. One evening, when the Prince was dining at Melbourne House, news was brought that an attack had been made on the life of George III, while he was watching a play at Drury Lane. The Prince, to whom the misfortunes of his parents were agreeable rather than otherwise, was preparing to go calmly on with his dinner. But Lady Melbourne perceived at once that he ought to go and enquire. It would make him popular, it would do him good with the King; it was, in any case, the correct thing to do. He resisted, she coaxed and ordered the carriage. At last sulkily he went off. But before midnight he had come back to thank her for her advice. Certainly for William, to stay at home was to see the world: and to get an education in public life thrown in.

Holland House and Devonshire House were educative

too; and in a more delightful wisdom. They represented, in their different ways, the apex of Whig civilization. In them all that made it memorable found its fullest expression. Holland House showed its masculine and intellectual side. Lady Holland was a divorced woman: she had eloped with Lord Holland from her first husband, Sir Godfrey Webster. With the consequence that, though the easy-going circle of Lady Melbourne and the Duchess of Devonshire were on terms with her, she was never received by the more rigid ladies; and the society that visited her was predominantly male. Every night of the week gentlemen used to drive down through the green fields of Kensington to dine and sleep at Holland House. Staying there had its drawbacks. It could be agonizingly cold for one thing; and the dinner table was always overcrowded, so that people ate as best they could, with arms glued to their sides. Moreover Lady Holland herself was in many respects a tiresome woman, capricious, domineering and extremely egotistic; given to a hundred deliberately cultivated fads, with which she expected everyone to fall in. She shifted her guests' places in the middle of a meal, she turned people out of the room for using scent, she interrupted, she had hysterics at a clap of thunder, suddenly she would summon an embarrassed stranger to her sitting-room in order that he might entertain her with conversation, while her page, Edgar, kneeling before her and with hands thrust beneath her skirts, rubbed her legs to alleviate rheumatism. Yet she was a good hostess; talked cleverly in a charmless combative style, and had the dominating vitality that keeps a party alive. It was Lord Holland, though, who attracted people to the house. With the bushy black brows, the clumsy figure of his uncle, Charles Fox—"in a white waistcoat," said a contemporary, "Lord Holland looks like a turbot standing on its tail"—he possessed also his culture, his bonhomie, his exquisite amenity of address. Perhaps he was a little detached— one needed to be, to live with Lady Holland—but this only seemed still further to emphasize the unvarying infectious good humour which spread like sunshine over every gathering of which he was host. Certainly life at Holland House had an extraordinary charm; there was nothing like it in Europe, people said. It was partly Lord Holland, partly the setting, the stately, red-brick, Jacobean mansion, with its carven painted rooms, mellow with historical memories; it was chiefly the conversation. Lady Holland complained that only men visited her; she complained of most things. But in fact it was this circumstance which gave the talk at her house its unique quality. It imbued it with that mental vigour found as a rule only in exclusively male society. The tone was free and sceptical, the subject matter rational and cultivated. There of an evening in the long library, soft in winter with candle shine, in summer fresh with the garden air blowing in through the open windows, would flow forth, concentrated and easy as it could never be in the rush of London life, the strength, the urbanity and the amplitude of Whig culture; passing from politics to history, from history to literature, Madame de Sévigné's letters, the controversies of the early Church, the character of Buonaparte; and then Lord Holland would set everyone laughing with an imitation of Lord Chatham— he was an even better mimic than the Prince of Wales— and then someone would raise a point of scholarship, and taking a folio from the shelves would verify a reference. The company was always intellectually distinguished. There were a few habitués, Mr. Allen, the librarian, erudite and positive, his eyes always bright behind his spectacles, to argue on behalf of atheism; Sydney Smith, most humane of clergymen, crackling away like a genial bonfire of jokes and good sense and uproarious laughter; the sardonic Rogers; the epigrammatic Luttrell. But most of the remarkable men of the age came there at one time or another, statesmen, writers, artists, distinguished foreigners. Lord and Lady Holland were always on the look out for new talent; and William's reputation soon got him an invitation. "William Lamb, a rising young genius, dines here for the first time to-day," notes Lady Holland in her diary, 1799. He made his usual impression; "pleasant though supercilious"; and later, "clever and agreeable and will improve when he gets over his love of singularity." He, for his part, appreciated them. In Holland House he discovered an intellectual life deeper than could be found at home. From this time on, whenever he came to London, he found time to pay it a visit. In the course of years he became a regular habitué whose association was only to be ended by death.

All the same it is to be doubted if he did not enjoy Devonshire House more. Here flowered the feminine aspect of Whiggism. The Duke, a stiff, shy man, preferred to follow his own way, aloof from others; and the social life of his home revolved round the Duchess, her sister Lady Bessborough, and her friend Lady Elizabeth Foster. Each, in her way, was conspicuously charming; the Duchess in particular, lovely, exuberant, her whole personality flushed with a glowing sweetness which no heart could resist, seemed born to get and to give pleasure. From the time she was eighteen, the great house gazing across its courtyard at Green Park was the scene of all that was gayest and most brilliant in London society. Life there had none of the ordered rationality of Holland House. It passed in a dazzling, haphazard confusion of routs, balls, card parties, hurried letter-writings, fitful hours of talk and reading. But in its own way it was also unique. Rare indeed it is to find a real palace inhabited by a real princess, a position of romantic wealth and splendour, filled by figures as full of glamour as itself. Moreover in Devonshire House, the graces were cultivated in the highest perfection. Here, in the flesh was the exquisite eighteenth century of Gainsborough, all flowing elegance, and melting glances and shifting silken colour. Its atmosphere was before all things personal. The characteristic conversation of the Devonshire House ladies was "tête-à-tête," in a secluded boudoir, or murmured in the corner of a sofa amid the movement of a party; it was delightful for its charming gaiety, its intimate sympathy, its quick perception of nuance. Their culture—for they too were cultivated— was of a piece with the rest of them, an affair of enthusiasm and sensibility. They read and wrote poems, they listened to music, they appreciated subtle analyses of emotion and character, LaNouvelle Héloise, Les Liaisons Dangereuses. In politics they were all for the ideal, for honour and liberty and enlightenment. Above everything they prized warmth and delicacy of feeling, abhorred cynicism, vulgarity and harshness. People spoke gently in Devonshire House, smiled rather than laughed, expressed disapproval, if they had to, by a hint or an intonation. Their less sensitive acquaintances criticized

59

them as sentimental and insincere; laughed at the gushing terms, interspersed at every turn with French phrases, in which they expressed themselves, their cooing ecstatic voices, "the Devonshire House drawl." But the Duchess and her sister, at any rate, were in reality the very reverse of artificial. They seemed affected because they were unself-conscious; their privileged position had always allowed them to express their naturally refined and warm-blooded temperaments with uninhibited freedom. Impulsive, spontaneous, uncontrolled, they followed in everything the mood of the moment, the call of the heart. They danced till dawn, they gambled wildly, they mourned and rejoiced with equal lack of restraint. In them the affections, for friends, for relations, swelled to fever pitch; while into love they flung themselves with a reckless abandon. Love was indeed their vocation, the centre and mainspring of their lives. From earliest youth to the threshold of old age, the ladies of Devonshire House had always an affair of the heart on hand; ranging from light flirtation to the most agonizing drama of passion. For privilege did not save them from suffering. How should it, blown about as they were by every gust of desire, and without the slightest vestige of self-control? The life of feeling does not make for happiness in this rough world. The very basis of Devonshire House life was complicated by it.

Lady Elizabeth Foster, a penniless grass widow, living
by her wits, and of a more designing character than her
friends, had, in addition to being the Duchess's friend,
contrived also to become the Duke's mistress. And
though a vigilant tact enabled them all to get along
together without open explosions, they lived at an un-
ceasing tension, rendered still sharper by the vicissitudes
of the Duchess's own hectic amours. At once gorgeous
and dishevelled, frivolous and tragic, life at Devonshire
House was a continual strain on the spirit; beneath its
shining surface seethed always a turmoil of yearning
and jealousy, crisis and intrigue, gnawing hope and
unavailing despair. All the same the source of its unrest
was also the chief secret of its attraction. For it meant
that it was quickened by that delicious emotional stir
only found in societies whose chief concern is love. It
was love that breathed warmth into the social arts in
which its inhabitants were so accomplished: love suffused
the atmosphere, in which they moved, with a soft enticing
shimmer of romantic sentiment and voluptuous grace.

William responded to it at once. His animal nature
and his taste for women's society united to make him
amorous: and natural tendency had been encouraged by
the tradition of his home. Already, we gather, he had
sown some wild oats. Like the other young men of his
circle he thought chastity a dangerous state: and he

seems early to have taken practical steps to avoid incur-
ring the risks attendant on it. But he never became a
regular habitué of the Regency demi-monde as his brothers did. He was at once too sensitive and too sophisticated to get much satisfaction from its boisterous revel-
lings, the showy seductions of its sirens. This was all
the more reason he should like Devonshire House. And
he did. Beside its civilized femininity even that of Lady
Melbourne looked crude: all the poetic and fastidious
elements in him sprang to it, as to something he had
always been seeking. It was not the Duchess herself so
much who attracted him. By the time he was grown
up, the wear and tear of her existence had begun to tell
on her; she was only the wreck of what she had been,
melancholy, abstracted, and with her figure gone. William found her kindly but inattentive. Nor did he suc-
cumb to the insinuating allurements of Lady Elizabeth
Foster. But he was immediately drawn to Lady Bessborough. It is not to be wondered at. For though her attraction was not so immediately compelling as that of the
Duchess in her prime, it was of a rarer and more lasting
quality. Alike her enthralling letters and her portrait—
with its slanting glance, its amused, pensive mouth, its
air of indescribable distinction—proclaim her to have been
one of the most enchanting creatures that have ever lived;
combining her sister's overflowing generosity of spirit, and

HENRIETTA SPENCER Countess of Bessborough
From a painting by Sir Joshua Reynolds in the
possession of Earl Spencer

a refinement of feeling, that years of dissipation failed to tarnish, with a vivid, responsive intelligence and an instinctive subtlety of the heart that enabled her to penetrate a friend's every mood and thought. Alas, no more to her than to the Duchess did her gifts bring happiness. She lacked those colder qualities which carry the Lady Melbournes of this world securely to prosperity. Too softhearted, too ungoverned, she could not take a firm line with herself or anyone else. With the result that her existence passed in a series of shattering emotional entanglements, and that she died with her reputation gone, and the dearest wish of her heart unsatisfied. "I must put down what I dare tell nobody," she noted in later years. "I should be ashamed were it not so ridiculous . . . in my fifty-first year I am courted, followed, flattered and made love to . . . thirty-six years, a pretty long life, I have heard and spoken that language, for seventeen years of it loved almost to idolatry the man who has probably loved me least of all of those that professed to do so— though once I thought otherwise." Lord Granville, to whom she devoted her life, whose career she had furthered against her own political opinions, and of whose very infidelities she had forced herself to become the sympathetic confidante, had never prized her at her true worth; and in the end had forsaken her to marry her niece. However, this was many years ahead yet; when

William got to know her, Lady Bessborough was still light-hearted enough. He was never seriously in love with her: but he paid her marked attention. And London soon recognized him as one of her established train of beaux. He was always supping at her house in Cavendish Square with Sheridan and Lord Holland and the rest of her admirers, or staying at her country villa at Roehampton where they spent delightful days walking, talking and reading aloud. One day at Brocket he met another member of the family. A flock of child visitors were playing about the house: the young Devonshires, and among them a skimpy, elf-like little figure with a curly blonde head, Lady Bessborough's daughter, Caroline. She was an extraordinary child: at one moment a wild tomboy, galloping bareback round the field, the next conversing on poetry and politics like a woman of forty, her whole being vibrant with an electric vitality which dominated any room she entered. Precociously susceptible to the influence of her environment, she was much concerned with love. William's black eyes and his celebrated oration on progress seemed to make him a worthy object of her choice; she conceived a violent fancy for him. In his turn he found her very engaging. She appealed to his particular taste both for little girls and for entertaining characters. At times, as he lounged back in his chair listening to the flow of her odd, impudent charming chatter, a more sentimental interest began to tinge his amusement. In four or five years what a paragon she seemed likely to become; more irresistible, because more original even than her mother. A captivating vision of the future fleeted before his musing eyes. "Of all the Devonshire House girls," he remarked half laughingly to a friend, "that is the one for me."

Meanwhile he was twenty-one and she fourteen, and he had to finish his schooling. In 1799 his four years at Cambridge came to an end: but Lady Melbourne still felt that something remained to be done. The Whig aristocracy had a high standard of education. Commonly they sent their children on the grand tour, after they had finished the ordinary academic course. But during the Napoleonic Wars this was impracticable: so it became the fashion for those young noblemen, whose minds seemed susceptible of further development, to be sent to one of the northern universities, famous at that time as leaders of all that was newest in philosophical and scientific thought. In the winter of 1799 therefore, William and Frederic proceeded for two winters to Glasgow: where they lodged with a distinguished philosopher, Professor Millar. It was an extraordinary contrast to the luxurious sophistication of the world they had left. Earnest, industrious and provincial, the rawboned inhabitants of Professor Millar's house passed their time in an ordered round of plain living and hard thinking. However, the Lambs threw themselves into their new surroundings with their customary sardonic zest. "There is nothing heard of in this house but study," writes Frederic to his mother, "though there is much idleness, drunkenness, etc., out of it as in most universities. We breakfast at half past nine, but I am roused by a stupid, silly, lumbering mathematician, who tumbles me out of bed at eight. During the whole of the day we are seldom out of the house or the lecture rooms for more than an hour, and after supper, which finishes a little after eleven, the reading generally continues till near two. Saturday and Sunday are holidays, on Monday we have examinations in Millar's lectures. Millar himself is a little jolly dog, and the sharpest fellow I ever saw. All the ladies here are contaminated with an itch for philosophy, and learning, and such a set of fools it never was my lot to see. William quotes poetry to them all day, but I do not think he has made any impression yet." Neither did they, nor the place they lived in, make any formidable impression on him. "The town is a damnable one and the dirtiest I ever saw," he said, "and as for the company and manners I do not see much different in them from the company and manners of any country town." Still he set himself to make the most of such compensations as he could find in his new surroundings. He dined out with the merchants of the town, where he thoroughly enjoyed the local custom of serving brandy with dinner; he gave rein to his passion for argument in a debating club where he became noted for his "caustic brilliance in reply"; and he absorbed himself in Professor Millar's philosophical ideas. So much so, that when he came to London in vacation he could talk of little else. This was not altogether approved of by his old friends. Lady Holland was critical; while Lord Egremont, whose interest in his career was noticeably paternal, became worried. It would be dreadful, he thought, if William turned into a doctrinaire prig. Lady Melbourne communicated these fears to William, who brushed them aside. Indeed, no one was less disposed to be a doctrinaire. Further, enriched as he was by the practical experience of mankind to be learnt in Melbourne House, he was not, except on purely intellectual subjects, impressed by the naïve and self-assured dogmatizings of the middle-class intelligentsia with whom he associated. Life had taught him—this is the advantage of living in the thick of things—always to relate thought to experience, to estimate theory in terms of its practical working. He might be a little wild in his political ideas; but he knew that statesmen were human beings, not embodied institutions. In consequence, he listened to his companions good-humouredly, but with an inner amusement that must have disconcerted them, had they realized it. "No place can be perfect," he told Lady Melbourne, "and the truth is, that the Scotch universities are very much calculated to make a man vain, important, and pedantic. This is naturally the case where there is a great deal of reading. . . . We have two fellows in the house with us, who think themselves, each of them, as wise as Plato and Aristotle put together, and asked, with a supercilious sort of doubt, whether Pitt is really a good orator, or Fox has much political knowledge. This will all wear off in time; though, to be sure, one of them is three and twenty and has been in France since the revolution . . . the other is an Irishman, about my age, who knew nothing before he came here last year, and who therefore thinks that nobody knows anything anywhere else. . . . You cannot have both the advantages of study and of the world together. The way is to let neither of them get too fast a hold of you, and this is done by nothing so well as by frequent changes of place, of persons and of companions."

These words show a remarkably mature judgment for twenty-one. And William was old for his age. Lady Melbourne, watching him arrive in London, at last to take up that active role on the stage of the world for which she had prepared him so assiduously, could feel her work was thoroughly done. She had reason to be satisfied with it.

He was, on the whole, all she thought a young man ought to be; handsome, agreeable, self-confident. Perhaps a shade too self-confident: William had not altogether outgrown his youthful intransigence; he still proclaimed his contempt for stupidity too openly. And his manners were not all she could have wished. "Although I have the highest opinion of your skill," she writes to Lady Holland about her sons, "yet I believe even you would find bringing them to what is called polish a very arduous undertaking." However, Lady Melbourne sympathized with his contempt; and manners to her were of small importance compared with the point of view that they expressed. William's point of view she found quite satisfactory. It would have been odd if she had not: for it was largely the same as her own. His ductile mind had been unable to resist the influence of a philosophy, exerted so continuously and so persuasively. Further, such experience of life as he had known had gone to confirm it. William early noticed that, if he differed from his mother about a character or a course of action, he generally turned out to be wrong. "My mother was the most sagacious woman I ever knew," he used to say in later years, "as long as she lived, she kept me straight." Her cynicism did not put him off. Clever young men like cynicism if it is agreeably presented. It makes them feel both bold and wise, imbues them with a sense of daring superiority to the timid gullible herd of common mankind. Like Lady Melbourne's, William's outlook was realistic and rational, thinking highly of the world's pleasures and poorly of its inhabitants; sensibly determined to adjust itself to life so as to be as comfortable as possible; cheerfully convinced that idealists—excepting always the Foxite Whigs—were fools or hypocrites. In the exuberance of his youth he expressed these opinions more explicitly than she did herself. "I do not like the dissenters," he remarked to her . . . "they are more zealous and consequently more intolerant than the established church. Their only object is power. If we are to have a prevailing religion let us have one that is cool and indifferent . . . toleration is the only good and just principle, and toleration for every opinion that could possibly be formed." It was not Lady Melbourne's habit to generalize in this fashion: she showed her religious views simply —by never going to church. But she would have agreed with every word William said.

All the same, she was not completely satisfied with him. His opinions, his demeanour, were all they should be; but there were elements in his character which she found baffling; what in her rare moments of irritation she called "his laziness and his selfishness." These were not quite the right words, but they meant something. Hidden beneath his exterior pliability lay a force impervious to her will. It arose from that other conflicting strain in his personality. Education had driven it underground; but had not been able to expel it. The romantic and the philosopher still stirred restlessly in the depths of his subconsciousness, colouring his reactions, disturbing his equilibrium. Now and again they rose to the surface, revealing themselves, as people noticed, in his conversation, with its sudden tears, its fitful moments of enthusiasm. They appeared more significantly in sporadic movements of antagonism towards his home. These were to be expected. In spite of its charms, life at Melbourne House had an ugly side. Its hard animalism, its rapacious worldliness, were bound to jar on a person of sensibility. Nor in that plain-spoken age were they concealed. "Your mother is a whore," shouted a Cambridge friend to George Lamb in the heat of an undergraduate quarrel. George knocked him down; but he cannot have failed to know that there was truth in the insult. William must have learned this truth early too. And though in theory he did not set much value on chastity, yet such a discovery about his own mother is generally upsetting to a sensitive boy; especially if, like William, he is temperamentally susceptible to the charm of innocence. Again—and here he had his brothers with him—he was irritated by the violence of Lady Melbourne's ambition for her children: loudly they protested that they wished she would sometimes let their careers alone. Still less did William like the hardness of her mockery; with the candour of his family he told her so. "Everybody has foibles from which no quarantine can purify them," he writes to her. "No resource remains but to make up your mind to put up with them . . . as to Lewis' way of laughing people out of them—which by the way you are sometimes a little inclined to adopt—it only confirms them—and makes the person ridiculed hate you into the bargain." The tone of this reproof is good-natured enough. And indeed none of these sources of irritation counted for much in themselves. But they accumulated in William to create a secret uneasiness which is the most striking evidence of his inner maladjustment. His prevailing state of mind when he first grew up was unusual for a man of his age. Except in politics he was all for caution, inactivity and putting up with things. Though happy, he was not hopeful. Beneath the smooth surface of his equanimity, had sown themselves the seeds of a precocious disillusionment.

His first acquaintance with the world encouraged their growth. Whig society was an entertaining place: but it did not foster sentimental illusions. Even Devonshire House life had its seamy side; at Carlton House and in the demi-monde, the seamy side was uppermost. William entered them with some shreds of the ingenuous idealism of youth still hanging round him. He soon lost them;

and he felt it. Once seizing a pen he poured forth his feelings in some verses to a friend.

A year has pass'd—a year of grief and joy—
Since first we threw aside the name of boy,
That name which in some future hour of gloom,
We shall with sighs regret we can't resume.
Unknown this life, unknown Fate's numerous shares
We launched into this world, and all its cares;
Those cares whose pangs, before a year was past,
I felt and feel, they will not be the last.
But then we hailed fair freedom's brightening morn,
And threw aside the yoke we long had borne;
Exulted in the raptures thought can give,
And said alone, we then began to live;
With wanton fancy, painted pleasure's charms,
Wine's liberal powers, and beauty's folding arms,
Expected joys would spring beneath our feet,
And never thought of griefs we were to meet.
Ah! Soon, too soon is all the truth displayed,
Too soon appears this scene of light and shade!
We find that those who every transport know,
In full proportion taste of every woe;
That every moment new misfortune rears;
That, somewhere, every hour's an hour of tears.
The work of wretchedness is never done,

And misery's sigh extends with every sun.
Well is it if, when dawning manhood smiled
We did not quite forget the simple child;
If, when we lost that name, we did not part
From some more glowing virtue of the heart;
From kind benevolence, from faithful truth,
The generous candour of believing youth,
From that soft spirit which men weakness call,
That lists to every tale, and trusts them all.
To the warm fire of these how poor and dead
Are all the cold endowments of the head.

Such moods seldom got the upper hand in him. And no one who met him seems to have noticed them. But they had their effect; his uneasiness persisted, was confirmed.

Indeed he had cause to be uneasy. Education, though it had muffled their clash, had done nothing to reconcile the opposing tendencies in his nature. One half of him still went out to the ideal, the romantic; the other told him that, in actual fact, self-interest and material satisfactions were the controlling motive forces in the world. As he grew older the struggle was further complicated by the fact that his personal and his ideal sympathies became engaged against each other. The people he was fondest of, all took the anti-ideal side. Yet he continued to respond to the call of his imagination as strongly as before. He was in an impasse.

It did not worry him very much. Life was pleasant, he was adaptable. Moreover, gradually and insensibly, he had evolved a mode of thought and action, by which he could evade the more distressing implications of his situation. He did not suppress his ideal instincts; there was an obstinate integrity in his disposition which made him incapable of denying anything he genuinely felt. But still less did he throw over his realism, to follow the call of his heart. He would have thought it silly, for one thing: his reason told him that his family's point of view was right. Besides, to quarrel with it would have entailed a row; and he hated rows. No more now than as an Eton boy did he see the sense of standing up to be knocked to pieces. As at Eton, therefore, he compromised; adopted a neutral, detached position, which enabled him to enjoy the world he lived in, while avoiding those of its activities which most violently outraged his natural feelings. He refused to be ambitious, to join in the sordid scuffle for place and power; he conducted his own personal relationships by a rigid standard of delicacy and honour; and he always said what he thought, regardless of public opinion. On the other hand he taught himself to tolerate other people's opinions; he lived the life that was expected of him; and he concentrated his heart and interests chiefly on those pleasures which his home did provide. Social life, public affairs, occupied a growing share of his attention: while his emotions attached themselves primarily to his personal affections. In them, indeed, both sides of his nature did, in some sort, find fulfilment. Love for a living individual was both real and romantic. It became the strongest motive power in his life. For the rest, though he indulged his taste for philosophizing, he was doubtful if it had any value. He was a sceptic in thought, in practice a hedonist. Shelving deeper problems, he enjoyed the passing moment wholeheartedly, and took his own character as little seriously as he could.

Such an attitude worked very well for the time being. It was easy to be a successful hedonist in the Whig society of 1800, if one was as popular and as cheerful as William. His faculty for self-adaptation worked as well as it had at school: he continued to be happy. All the same he paid a heavy price for his happiness. His condition of mind was not a healthy one. Resting as it did on an unresolved discord, its basic foundation was insecure. This insecurity was increased by the bias given to his outlook by upbringing. In spite of all her wisdom and all her affection, it was a pity that Lady Melbourne was his mother. His view of life, if it was to be a stable affair, must be built, in part at least, on his ideal sentiments. Lady Melbourne's opinions, and still more her example, tended to make him distrust these. In her smooth efficient way she had managed to discredit his best feelings in his own eyes. And even if he was unaware of the cause, it made him feel uneasy all the time.

Nor was the philosophy he had adopted to meet the difficulties of his situation good for him. It is unnatural to be a materialist, when one is twenty-three years old and throbbing with idealistic feelings. And the efforts William was forced to make to maintain himself in his scepticism, against the pull of his nature, produced a sort of frustration in his character. He grew far too self-preservative, for one thing. Insecurely perched in his little patch of tranquil neutrality, he became dominated by the desire to preserve it from invasion. His hatred of trouble grew stronger and stronger, till he would make practically any sacrifice to avoid an unpleasant scene, to put off a difficult decision. It modified even his attitude to those personal relationships by which he set such store. Though he was unfailingly considerate and unselfish in little things, he never dreamt of letting his feeling for someone he loved divert him from the course of life he had marked out for himself: still less would he take the responsibility of guiding their lives. An enlightened policy of live and let live was his method of running a relationship.

But beyond this, his upbringing had a more formidable, a more disastrous effect upon him. It crippled the development of his most valuable faculties. These were intellectual. Nature had meant him for that rare phenomenon, a philosophical observer of mankind. His detachment and his curiosity, his honesty and his perceptiveness, his sense of reality and his power of generalization, all these mingled together to make his mind of the same type, if not of the same high quality, as that of Montaigne or Sir Thomas Browne: the mind of the botanist in the tangled jungle of men and their thoughts, exploring, observing, classifying. But to be a thinker, one must believe in the value of disinterested thought. William's education had destroyed his belief in this, along with all other absolute beliefs; and in so doing, removed the motive force necessary to set his creative energy working. The spark that should have kindled his fire was unlit: with the result that he never felt moved to make the effort needed to discipline his intellectual processes, to organize his sporadic reflections into a coherent system of thought. He had studied a great many subjects, but none thoroughly; his ideas were original, but they were fragmentary, scattered, unmatured. This lack of system meant further that he never overhauled his mind to set its contents in order in the light of a considered standard of value. So that the precious and the worthless jostled each other in its confused recesses: side by side with fresh and vivid thoughts lurked contradictions, commonplaces,

78

and relics of the conventional prejudices of his rank and station. Even his scepticism was not consistent; though he doubted the value of virtue, he never doubted the value of being a gentleman. Like so many aristocratic persons he was an amateur.

His amateurishness was increased by his hedonism. For it led him to pursue his thought only in so far as the process was pleasant. He shirked intellectual drudgery. Besides, the life he lived was all too full of distracting delights. If he felt bored reading and cogitating, there was always a party for him to go to, where he could be perfectly happy, without having to make an effort. Such temptations were particularly hard to resist for a man brought up in the easy-going disorderly atmosphere of Melbourne House; where no one was ever forced to be methodical or conscientious, and where there was always something entertaining going on. If virtue was hard to acquire there, pleasure came all too easily. Merely to look on kept one contented.

Indeed that was the danger. At twenty-one William was already an onlooker; an active-minded, lively onlooker, ready to respond to every thrill, every joke in the drama: but standing a little aloof, without any compelling desire to take part himself. He had made his peace with the world, and on favourable terms: but none the less the world had, in this first round of the fight, defeated him.

Endowed by birth with one of the most distinguished minds of his generation, there was a risk that he might end as nothing more than another charming ineffective Whig man of fashion.

A risk but not a certainty: William's character had taken shape but it was not yet set into its final mould. And the rebellious elements within it still surged, seeking an outlet. At moments, as we have seen, they burst out in his talk: his Foxite idealism still sounded, a discordant trumpet note, in the minor harmony of his scepticism: even his intellectual arrogance was the sign of a spirit not yet resigned to accept life just as he found it. A change of circumstance, the pressure of a new influence, and there was a chance he might yet, in some later engagement, turn the tables on the world; that his creative energy, gathering its forces together, might break through the inhibitions induced by upbringing, and gush forth to fulfilment. There was still a chance.

PART II

Chapter III

LOVE

OR a year or two his career marked time. There was a little uncertainty at first as to what profession he should adopt. He had been destined for the bar; but now Lady Melbourne suddenly suggested he should become a clergyman. It was a curious idea, considering that he doubted Christian doctrines and disapproved of Christian morals. But the Whig aristocracy did not regard faith as an essential qualification for holy orders. To them the church was primarily a good profession for younger sons. William's scholarly tastes and relatively discreet private character seemed to make him especially fitted for it; with any reasonable luck he should be a bishop before he died. However, he did not show any

83

enthusiasm for the proposal; and Lord Egremont was flat against it. Turning therefore to the secular world, Lady Melbourne sat down and wrote to the Prince of Wales asking him for a job for William in connection with the Office of the Stannaries. The Prince replied with a refusal, in which the fulsome effusiveness of his language was only equalled by the obvious strength of his determination to do nothing at all. In the end it was settled that, after all, William should become a lawyer. He was quite willing. Going on circuit was a new experience; he found himself, as usual, pleasantly popular with his fellow barristers; it gave him a thrill of delighted pride to be offered his first brief. Still, law did not rouse his interest sufficiently to divert him from his chosen career of leisure and pleasure. He continued to write verses and prologues to private theatricals; he went to Carlton House and Roehampton more than ever; and he often found time to go down to the country for "a bath of quiet," reading and day-dreaming. In any case, after a few years, an event took place that made his indolence of little account. In January, 1805, Peniston Lamb died of consumption. For the moment all was forgotten in sorrow. On so devoted a family the blow fell with extraordinary force; Lady Melbourne herself was so overcome by emotion as even to forget her usual worldly preoccupations. Openly disregarding public opinion she had invited Peniston's mistress, the pretty Mrs. Dick Musters, to stay at Melbourne House that she might soothe his last moments; when he died Lady Melbourne was desolated. For William the event was momentous. His prospects were entirely reversed; he was now the heir to a peerage and a large fortune. It was not in reality anything to be thankful for. He was now, even more inextricably than before, entangled in the web of that worldly life which, since he was a child, had hampered him in following the best course for his talents. As a younger son there was no practical reason—if he had ever felt the inclination—why he should not break away from conventional exist-ence and devote himself to that life of thought and writing in which he could most fully have expressed him-self. But future peers in that day were not free. They were integral and active parts of the great machine of aristocratic government and social life; to them, almost as much as to a royal prince, was allotted a ready-made role, function, responsibilities. For them, to take up a life of contemplation was to act in opposition to the whole pressure and tradition of the society of which they were members. It was made all the more difficult by the fact that the position imposed on them was such an attractive one. With some of the duties of royalty they had all its pleasures and privileges. They walked through life en-vied by men and courted by women, recognized and acclaimed monarchs of a magnificent realm. Certainly William seems to have felt no qualm on accepting his new position. No more at this juncture than in earlier days, did he show the slightest conscious realization that the life to which he was called diverted him from his true bent. He took it for granted, for instance, that like other eldest sons, he must now go into the House of Commons. The only problem that worried him was what seat he should stand for. Should it be Leominster or Hertford? He went down to Hertford and delighted his supporters with an excellent speech. But for some reason he preferred Leominster. In October, 1805, he was elected member. But before this he had taken a more irrevocable step. He had married.

Ever since 1802 he had wanted to. In that year Caroline Ponsonby, now a grown-up young lady of seventeen, was launched on the world. She had matured into all and more than all that William could have hoped for. Indeed she was the most dynamic personality that had appeared in London society for a generation. Outwardly she had hardly changed since he first met her. Slight, agile, and ethereal, with a wide-eyed wilful little face, and curly short hair, she still looked a child; like something less substantial even,—"the Sprite," people called her, "the Fairy Queen, Ariel." Her fresh lisping voice, too, trained though it was to linger cooingly on the syl-

LADY CAROLINE LAMB
*From a water colour sketch in the possession of
the Marquis of Crewe*

lables in the approved Devonshire House manner, was a child's voice; "Lady Caroline," said an irritated rival, "baas like a little sheep." Nor did her exterior belie what lay within. As much as at fourteen she still loved to gallop bareback, to dress up in trousers, to lose herself in day-dreams; when the fit took her she screamed and tore her clothes in ungovernable rage. No one could have been less like the conventional idea of a young lady. On fire for the dramatic, the picturesque, the ideal, openly at war with the tame and the trivial, at every turn she flouted convention; would rush into the street dressed anyhow, spoke her mind with *enfant terrible* candour, plunged straight into the subjects which interested her, regardless of the formalities of polite conversation. As for orthodox feminine employments, gossip, embroidery, they filled her with ineffable contempt. More normal girls like her cousin Harriet Cavendish, not unnaturally resented this. In fact, many people thought her tiresome; even her friends admitted she was difficult. Yet they forgave her everything. The Fairy Queen cast a spell, which, for those on whom it worked, was not to be resisted. It came partly from the sheer spontaneous intensity of her temperament. In each changing mood, her gusts of irresponsible gaiety, the trembling sensibility which responded like a violin string to poetry, music, eloquence, she seemed more alive than

87

other people; and heightened their sense of life by her presence. She was very clever too, in a fitful, darting way. Too impatient to follow a logical process, and generally in the clouds, she could yet on occasion pierce to the heart of a subject with a lightning insight that dazzled her hearers. And she expressed herself with a direct vividness of phrase which made her every word memorable. But beyond all this, beyond her gifts and her vitality, there was in her a touch of something stranger and more precious—was it genius?—a creative individuality, whimsical, extravagant, enchanting, which scrawled its signature in a thousand fanciful flourishes on everything she said or did. Sometimes it blossomed forth in an Elizabethan fantasy of humour, "my most sanative elixir of julep, my most precious cordial confection," so she begins a letter to a cousin thanking him for a medical prescription; the same quality flitted in zig-zag butterfly flights across her most sombre confessions of melancholy. "I am like a vestal who thought of other concerns than the poor flame she hoped Heaven would keep burning. Do not condemn me to be burnt alive; wait a little, I shall return to dust without any unusual assistance": or "I go off ... and you will probably see among the dead in some newspaper—died on her voyage, Lady Caroline Lamb, of the disease called death; her time being come and she being a predestinarian"; she cannot recommend a governess without it breaking out; "Miss X. is sensible, handsome, young, good, unsophisticated, independent, true, ladylike, above any deceit or meanness, romantic, very punctual about money; but she has a cold and a cough and is in love. I cannot help it, can you?" This spirit thrusts its irrepressible head into the very datings of her letters: "Brocket Hall, heaven knows what day," thus she heads a formal congratulation to a prospective sister-in-law she has not yet met. Here we come to the secret of her peculiar spell. Lady Melbourne might be more brilliant, the Duchess of Devonshire more winning, Lady Bessborough more intimately lovable; but where in them is to be found this bewitching unexpectedness, this elusive gleam lit at the very torch of will-o'-the-wisp?

William was born to be her victim. His sceptical, sophisticated spirit was at once entertained and invigorated by her naturalness and her certainty: his repressed idealism glowed, even against his better judgment, in response to the confidence of hers; and he appreciated her unique flavour, with the discriminating relish of the connoisseur in human nature that he was. If he were to live a hundred years, he knew, he would find no one else like this. All the force of his virile, tender nature went out to her; he fell irretrievably in love. For the time being it had to be a hopeless love. The social conventions of the day made it unthinkable that Lord Bessborough's only daughter should throw herself away on a younger son of small fortune. William was too unselfish and too sensible to involve Caroline in the fruitless unhappiness that must ensue from an attempt to combat universal custom. Though he could not altogether conceal his feelings, he never declared himself formally; and made some ineffective efforts to fall in love with other people. Caroline returned his passion, but oddly enough for one of her character, she also submitted to convention. Anyway, she told him, it would be a bad thing for them to marry; she was too much of a fury. Could not she, as an alternative, she suggested, accompany him on circuit disguised as a clerk? Meanwhile other young men, her cousins, Lord Althorp and Lord Hartington, were paying court to her; it seemed probable she would end by marrying one of them. For a year or two her relations with William remained, outwardly at least, no more than a fashionable flirtation.

Peniston's death put the situation on a new footing. Even now William was a less brilliant match than she might have anticipated; at least till his father died. For on his eldest son's death Lord Melbourne had, for the only recorded time in his history, cut up rough. The accumulated mortifications of thirty years boiled over; he refused point blank to allow William the £5,000 a year

he had bestowed on the indisputably legitimate Peniston.
So strongly did he express himself on the subject that
Lady Melbourne actually lost her nerve. Too scared to
approach him herself, she was reduced to asking a friend
to persuade him to reconsider his decision. In vain; Lord
Melbourne was adamant, and William had to make do
with £2,000 a year. Still £2,000 a year, with the Melbourne fortune in prospect, was good enough. In May,
when the first months of mourning were over, William
wrote a letter to Caroline in which he poured forth his
pent up emotions. "I have loved you for four years, loved
you deeply, dearly, faithfully—so faithfully that my love
has withstood my firm determination to conquer it when
honour forbade my declaring myself—it has withstood
all that absence, variety of objects, my own endeavours
to seek and like others, or to occupy my mind with fixed
attention to my profession, could do to shake it." There
was little doubt as to what Caroline's answer would be.
But her family's attitude was not yet quite certain. It was
not the marriage Lady Bessborough would have chosen.
The Lamb spirit had always been unsympathetic to her;
she was peculiarly repelled by cynicism, coarseness, and
off-hand manners; even in William, she was jarred by his
"creed or rather no creed" as she put it. As for Lady
Melbourne, though she had known her for years, she
had never been able to feel easy in her company. Far

too acute not to see through her suave exterior, she yet shrank too much from friction to be able to stand up to her. Beside Lady Melbourne's finished poise she felt herself continually at a disadvantage; she called her the Thorn. On the other hand, she liked William personally very much; she knew Caroline to be passionately in love with him. And she was anxious to get her off her hands as soon as she could. Caroline was altogether too temperamental for family life: and was sometimes so disagreeable in her manner that Lady Bessborough had come to the conclusion that only the settling influence of marriage would ever cool her down. Anyway she was not the woman to stand in the path of true love. Sighing, she left the matter to Caroline's decision. A day or two later William was asked to come to the play with the Bessborough's, in order to receive his final answer:

"We met him at Dy. Lane," Lady Bessborough tells Lord Granville, "I never saw anything so warm and animated as his manner towards her, and of course he soon succeeded in obtaining every promise he wished. I had not seen him to speak to, and he follow'd me into the passage (behind the D. Lane box). I was very nervous, and on telling him I knew Lord B. join'd with me in leaving everything to Caro's decision, he answered: 'And that decision is in my favour, thank heaven!' and so saying, threw his arms round me and kiss'd me. At that very moment I look'd up and saw the Pope* and Mr. Hammond before me in the utmost astonishment. W. frighten'd at their appearance, started back and ran downstairs. No words can paint to you my confusion, but, unable to bear the Pope's mortifying conjectures even till all was declar'd, I flew after him and calling him out, told him the cause of what he saw, and you can have no conception of his kindness; he was delighted, quieted all my fears, assur'd me my objections were Idle—prais'd William extremely, and did me more good than any one thing I had heard before. He touch'd me to that degree with his kindness that I could not resist pressing his hand to my lips (I hope it was not wrong?)"

The experience of the next few weeks confirmed the Pope's praises. William, now received as a son into the intimacy of the home circle, revealed to the full his genius for affection; Caroline, too, grew surprisingly more serene, once she was engaged. A delicious relationship established itself among the three of them, rosy with tenderness, sparkling with graceful gaiety.

* A nickname for Canning.

"Your letter made me cry," Lady Bessborough writes to Caroline, "and then laugh at myself for crying. The truth is we are two simpletons, and unlike what mother and daughter ought to be—William may pride himself on his good conduct; for to nothing one atom less kind and delightful than he is, could I have yielded you. I should have forbid the banns at last, with anybody else; but as I told you the other day, he really appears to me like my *natural son*—I shall hasten to do your commission; for I know your happiness cannot be compleat without Rollin's ancient History, that dear beautiful light amusing book. What a pity that it should be in twenty-four volumes and in quarto, that you cannot carry it always about you—could not you contrive a little rolling bookcase, you might draw after you, containing these precious volumes? I do not despair of your being soon able to repeat the whole, heads of chapters and all; how lulling it will be for William when he is a little drowsy. The book on education seems to me rather premature: but I will get it. What Prince do you intend to marry your future daughter to? Some of the Buonaparte family perhaps, that I may have the pleasure of being Grandmother to an Empress."

All the same the wedding did not pass off without its

storms. Lord Hartington, when the Bessboroughs came round to Devonshire House with the news, was seized with such paroxysms of agitation at the loss of his love, that a doctor had to be summoned. Then, the Thorn proved as thorny as Lady Bessborough could have feared. The antipathy between the two mothers-in-law was mutual. To Lady Melbourne, Lady Bessborough's virtues and faults were alike distasteful; sensitive, enthusiastic, imprudent persons were the type she had always found most tiresome; and she thought the gushing manner with which Lady Bessborough sought to conceal the nervousness she felt in her presence, both silly and insincere. To these original sources of irritation was now added jealousy. Though she approved his marriage from the worldly point of view, Lady Melbourne could not bear to see her adored William so obviously absorbed in two other women. In the exhausting rush of wedding preparations her exasperation betrayed itself:

"Yesterday, after various very unpleasant *cuts*," says Lady Bessborough, "she told me she hoped the Daughter would turn out better than the Mother, or William might have to repent of his choice; and would not (like many Husbands) be made to repent impunément. This was said half joke, half earnest; but there are subjects too sore to bear a joke.... I felt hurt and possibly could have retorted, but check'd myself, however; and only said I hoped and believ'd she would prove much better—'especially (I added) with the help of your advice' (I would not say example)."

Unluckily, too, as the ceremony approached, Caroline became herself again. The strain of buying a trousseau and her alarm at the thought of leaving her family for the first time, united to disperse her unwonted calm. She was attacked with moods of tearful melancholy, which on the actual wedding-day rose to hysteria. They were married at eight o'clock in the evening in Cavendish Square. Towards the end of the service Caroline, seized by an unaccountable fit of rage with the officiating bishop, tore her gown and was carried fainting from the room. An hour later, as she drove off through the summer dusk for her honeymoon at Brocket under the gaze of a huge crowd, she was still in a violent nerve storm. However, she was in good hands. William had been stirred by this, the first powerful emotional experience of his lifetime, to break free from his customary attitude of amiable detachment. During the ceremony his manner was remarked on as "beautiful, so tender and considerate"; once married, he took complete charge of her. On his own responsibility he opened her letters, only allowing her to see them if they contained nothing to distress her; he asked Lady Bessborough not to visit her till she had got over her home-sickness; and himself superintended her day with vigilant care. Indeed his marriage released his nature in more ways than one. The new atmosphere of delicate demonstrative emotion in which he found himself, thawed the Lamb reserve. Shyly, tentatively, and with a stiffness still far removed from Devonshire House rhapsodizings, he tried to be demonstrative too. "I am very bad at making professions," he writes to his grand-mother-in-law, Lady Spencer, "and have besides an invincible aversion to them, but believe me I shall be very happy to come to Holywell, the moment Caroline says she wishes it, and to stay there, as long as you will allow us; and this not only now, when I may be supposed to act so for the sake of appearance, but at any time and at all times in future—notwithstanding what I have said above about professions I cannot help acknowledging that I feel the greatest and sincere satisfaction in my dear Caroline's love and respect for you." And later we find him beginning a letter to her: "My dearest Love, since you do not like the other opening." What the other opening was is unknown; but clearly it was insufficiently demonstrative. However, during the honeymoon he showed affection enough for his immediate purpose. His mingled tenderness and good sense made him the ideal person to soothe disordered nerves. In the mornings,

97

with Caroline clinging to his arm, they walked the glades of Brocket park, drowsy in the June sunshine: later in the day she sketched, while he read aloud. Within a few weeks Caroline was sufficiently recovered to throw herself into the delights of fulfilled love with all the intensity of her nature.

Chapter IV

MARRIAGE

FOR THE next three years they lived in a state of idyllic happiness. Not that they secluded themselves from the world. On the contrary they were one of the smartest young couples in London. Their home was in the heart of its whirling centre: Lady Melbourne, in the Continental fashion, had allotted to them the first floor of the family mansion in Whitehall. Here, attended by a retinue of pages in liveries of scarlet and sepia designed by Caroline, they kept open house; received morning and afternoon visitors; gave dinner parties lasting till one in the morning, after which the guests would sometimes descend to Lady Melbourne's apartments on the ground floor for supper. Two years after marriage a son was born, Augustus.

"Caroline was brought to bed about an hour ago of a very large boy for so small a woman," wrote William to Lady Holland with paternal jocoseness. Caroline's own emotions were of so lyrical a kind as to require verse for their expression.

"His little eyes like William's shine—
How then is great my joy,
For while I call this darling mine,
I see 'tis William's boy."

To celebrate the christening, Lady Melbourne gave a magnificent party. Melbourne House was illuminated outside and in; and a huge concourse of guests, headed by the Prince of Wales, entertained themselves with eating and drinking and composing rhymes. The young Lambs spent as much time out as at home. They were to be seen everywhere: at the opera, at Drury Lane, at Almack's; staying with the Duke of Gloucester at Cowes, taking part in theatricals at Lord Abercorn's country house—William, who appeared in the role of Captain Absolute, was remarked on as "rather too vehement but very gentleman-like and nothing bad"—and very often at Devonshire House, where scandal had it that Caroline was once carried in concealed under a silver dish cover, from which she emerged on the dinner table, stark naked,

to the consternation of the company. We have glimpses
of William alone, too; at Brooks's Club, to which he had
been introduced by Fox himself, and staying at Brocket
in order to take part in the exercises of the local yeo-
manry. At such times Caroline, left to herself, drew,
danced and improved her mind by serious reading. In
her enthusiasm she summoned others to assist her.

"My dear Mama," she writes in July, 1809, "if you are
quite well, I should take it as a great favour if you would
just write me the principal dates and events, wars, risings
from Romulus till the time of Constantine the Great—if
you are unwell do not do it."

Poor Lady Bessborough! she must have needed to be
healthy indeed to perform such a task at the height of
the London season. Caroline was equally interested in
contemporary history; she and William had the Whig
taste for public affairs. Every important event of that
dramatic epoch stirred them; the Battle of Copenhagen,
the Peninsular Campaign, the death of Pitt. This last,
one might have expected to leave William unmoved, considering the unfavourable opinion he had always entertained of that statesman's policy. But the passing of so
historic a figure kindled his inflammable imagination; all
Pitt's faults were forgotten in the flow of generous emotion that welled up within him; moving him in fact to an
uncharacteristic and slightly comical sententiousness.

"When W. Lamb came in and told me," relates Lady Bessborough, "the tears were in his eyes too: and as I had drawn my veil over my face, he said, 'Do not be ashamed of crying: that heart must be callous indeed that could hear of the extinction of such a man unmoved. He may have erred but his transcendent talents were an honour to England and will live in posterity.'"

As for the way that people began canvassing as to who should get Pitt's seat at Cambridge, before he was cold in his grave, William thought it absolutely disgusting. "Damn him," he exclaimed vehemently, on receiving a note from one of the Whig leaders asking for his vote, "can no feeling but party enter his cold heart?": and he crumpled the note in his hand. It was a sad year altogether. Fox died soon after Pitt; and a few months earlier, after a protracted and agonizing illness, the Duchess of Devonshire. To her immediate circle it was an irreparable loss. With her went the centre round which their whole social life had revolved for thirty years, Caroline was plunged into an agony of tears; while Lady Bessborough's spirits received a shock from which they were never to recover.

However, neither private nor public calamities had the power to shake the inner citadel of the young Lambs' happiness. Love breathed round them a rosy cloud in which they moved, entrancedly insulated from the world.

TWO DRAWINGS OF WILLIAM LAMB and one of
the 1st Viscount Melbourne
*A leaf from the sketch book of Lady Caroline Lamb in the
possession of the Lady Desborough*

"They flirt all day," said an observer. And they talked as much as they flirted. William had always liked to teach, Caroline to be taught. Entertaining, unpedantic, his mind a storehouse of varied information, he was a perfect teacher; her quickness, her responsive enthusiasm, made her the ideal pupil. Every day of their crowded lives they contrived somehow to find time to read together; history, poetry, theology. Even in the turmoil of the Abercorn theatricals, she would write:

"Wm. and I get up about ten or half after or later (if late at night)—have our breakfast—talk a little—read Newton on the Prophecies with the Bible, having finished Sherlock—then I hear him his part, he goes to eat and walk—I finish dressing and take a drive or a little walk —then come upstairs where Wm. meets me and we read Hume with Shakespeare till the dressing bell."

When he was away he would send her translations from the classics he had made to pass the time, and ask her opinion of them: meanwhile she read the books he recommended that she might ply him with questions when he came back. And when they grew weary of serious subjects they would relax, she to enjoy his shrewd, subtle agreeability, he to savour her ever changing moods, the leaps and somersaults of her harlequin fancy. Whether serious or frivolous or sentimental, each was a continual delight to the other.

103

But it was not to last; their happiness was as shortlived as it was ecstatic. Before four years were over, a rift had begun to show itself in their relationship which was to bring down their married life in irreparable ruin. It was predominantly Caroline's fault. In spite of all her charms and all her talents, her character was of a kind to make her an unsatisfactory wife for any man. Not that it was a bad one. On the contrary, nature had made her generous, tender-hearted, fearless and unworldly. She aspired far more genuinely than most people to live a noble life; if her heart was touched, no kindness was too much trouble for her. But with a glint of the unique fire of genius, she possessed in the highest degree its characteristic defect. A devouring egotism vitiated every element in her character. In her eyes she was the unquestioned centre of the universe. She did not acknowledge, she was not even aware of any authority beyond her own inclinations. What she liked was right; what she disliked was wrong. This made her abnormally selfish, abnormally uncontrolled, and abnormally unreliable. One moment she would offer you her whole fortune, the next fly at you with nails and fists. In either mood she thought she was justified, and other people had to think so too. In addition, they had to admire her. Life was a drama in which she was cast as heroine; and both her fellow actors and her audience were expected to applaud her every movement. Capricious in all else, in one thing she was consistent, her determination to hold the centre of the stage. It was for this she dressed and behaved unlike other people; this was the reason of her faintings and sobbings and unconventional interruptions. Even her generous actions were partly a method of showing off. She liked to dazzle others by the spectacle of her munificence. For—it was the most dangerous effect of her egotism—her emotions were never completely sincere. It would be inaccurate to call her deceitful. Her very lack of control made her incapable of conscious pretence; indeed she thought quite sincerely that, compared with herself, most people were shocking hypocrites. But self-absorption tainted the essential quality of her reactions. Her feelings were one part genuine, two parts self-indulgent pleasure in emotion for its own sake, and three parts a means of self-glorification. Her intensest affections, her most exalted enthusiasms, were largely make-believe.

False feelings lead to a false vision of the world. "Truth," she said, "is what one believes at the moment." What she believed was always something creditable to herself. Since it was essential for her to see herself in the sympathetic light appropriate to a heroine, she learnt to blind herself to all facts that went against her, and to invent such others as were needed to set her conduct in a favourable perspective. Her history, as it appears in the records left to us, is an ironical comedy of appearance and reality. Side by side run always two stories, what happened to Caroline and what she pretended had happened. Living wholly in a wish-fulfilment world of her own creation, she insisted it was the real one. Nor was she content simply to contemplate its perfections. In order to feel completely satisfied, she had to impose the false world on the real. Disgusted with life as she found it, she was yet confident it could be made what she wished, and spent all her energies seeking out occasions and creating situations in which her dreams could be realized. Of course they proved a disappointment, but undefeated she always tried again. Her career was a series of theatrical performances designed to exhibit the brilliance of her personality to herself and the world. The agility of her imagination made her repertory of parts a large one. Comedy and tragedy came equally easy to her: sometimes she appeared as an unconventional child of nature, sometimes as an experienced woman of the world, sometimes as a devoted wife and mother; she was also ready to take the boards as a queen of fashion, or an heroic idealist. And it must be owned that in all these parts she gave a brilliant performance. Here was where her touch of genius came in. However commonplace the character she was impersonating, it was transfigured into something unique by her wit, her eloquence, the flicker of her fascinating fancy. We of posterity, watching her from the comfortable distance of a hundred years, feel inclined to applaud such masterpieces of the histrionic art with unqualified admiration. But it was very different for the people who had to live with her. For they had to behave as if she were not acting; they were required to respect and sympathize with sentiments they knew were mostly imaginary. Moreover, Caroline made use of them to fill the supporting roles in her productions; to their bewilderment, unasked and unrehearsed, they found themselves being treated as heroes and villains in dramas, of whose very plots they were ignorant. Sometimes, exasperated by some particularly flagrant example of her insincerity, they told her the truth about herself. Then for a moment the mask did fall; appearances were forgotten in a spitfire explosion of wounded vanity. But it was not for long. Within a short time the old machinery of self-deception began to work: she would re-enter as some new character designed to meet her new situation; it might be a pathetic penitent or a generous nature quick to recognize its faults; complete in either case with such plausible misrepresentation of the facts as was needed to give verisimilitude to the part she had chosen.

The extraordinary thing is that she should have been able to keep herself so blissfully blind to reality during nineteen years' existence on this disillusioning planet. But circumstances had been favourable to her. Her upbringing for one thing; Lady Bessborough, for all that she was so affectionate, was a bad mother. Unable to say no, and distracted by the complications of her own private life, she did nothing to check the extravagance of her daughter's temperament. Besides, her own reputation was so tarnished that it was thought better that Caroline should spend most of her childhood away from her; partly with her grandmother, Lady Spencer, and partly at Devonshire House. Neither did her much good. Lady Spencer found her at ten years old already such an unmanageable bundle of nerves that she sent for a doctor. He, anticipating Madame Montessori, opined that discipline was likely to injure so sensitive a child; she must be allowed to do whatever she liked. This régime produced the results any sensible person might have predicted. Caroline grew worse than ever. Nor was Devonshire House the environment to put her right. There the children were alternately spoiled and neglected. Now and again they were sent for to come to the drawing-room to be petted and made to show off; but for most of the time they roamed about the great house unruled and uncared for, eating only off silver plate, but lucky if they got their meals at all. Their existence was utterly out of touch with that of ordinary humanity. Caroline relates that she grew up thinking bread and butter grew on trees and that the population of the world was composed half of dukes and half of beggars; and though like everything she said this was an exaggeration, yet it did contain a truth. Aristocratic Devonshire House was not the place to acquire a sense of reality.

Finally, the philosophy to be learnt there encouraged her in all her failings. It set no value on reason or self-restraint; on the contrary, it insisted that passion and sensibility were the only virtues, that man should be guided in everything by the instinctive movements of his heart. Caroline embraced with enthusiasm a creed so consonant with her predilections. Indeed it was the determining factor in her development, for it decided the principal form her day-dreams were to take. Of her many roles, the one she assumed oftenest and with most satisfaction to herself was that of the romantic heroine; reckless and imprudent, the creature of her emotions, but sensitive, imaginative and nobly superior to the conventions that ruled pettier lives; living always in an intoxicating whirl of tragedy, ecstasy, passion and renown. The object of her whole life was to achieve an existence in which this conception of herself could be realized.

Such a character was bound to make a bad wife. Marriage demands precisely the qualities in which she was most deficient: dependability, forbearance, above all a sense of reality. It is impossible for two people to live on such intimate terms without discovering the truth about each other's character: and unless they are ready to accept that truth, they will never get on. Caroline, unable to understand William and furious if he understood her, inevitably quarrelled with him. Further, dissatisfied as she always was by actuality, she grew soon dissatisfied with the actualities of wedded life. She loved William as much as she could love anybody except herself, and at first she found she could fulfil her dreams by playing the unaccustomed roles of his wife and pupil. But when the glamour of novelty wore off, to be succeeded by the light of common day, she grew restless and discontented.

This discontent was increased by the environment in which she now lived. The Lambs were the last people with whom she could feel at home. She was flustered by their loud voices, offended by their casual manners, and shocked by their cynicism. Their penetration made her vanity uneasy; and their common-sense was always bringing her down to earth with an uncomfortable bump. Worst of all, the atmosphere they created was one in which she felt herself unable to shine. The Lambs did not believe in heroines and had no taste for whimsicality. Temper and insincerity on the other hand were to them the most unpardonable of faults. Indeed they found their new relation maddening. "What is the eleventh commandment?" she once asked George Lamb. "Thou shalt not bother," he replied in a spasm of exasperation. Among themselves the brothers and sisters alluded to her frankly as "the little beast." Even Lord Melbourne complained that she fidgeted; as for Lady Melbourne, she found Caroline even more tiresome than her mother. Two dominating personalities both absorbed in the same man, the relations between them were bound to be strained. But they could not have got on in any circumstances. Earth and fire, sense and sensibility, realism and fantasy, the eighteenth century and the nineteenth, each was in every respect the other's antithesis; Lady Melbourne, whose first principle it was to accept facts, Caroline, who rejected such few facts as she managed to recognize. Within a short time of William's marriage, war had broken out between them, which was to last till death. The battle swayed this way and that. In open combat Caroline was worsted; she had not the self-command to conduct an engagement with any tactics. Lady Melbourne took every advantage of her opponent's mistakes; crafty and relentless, she contrived to put her even more in the wrong than she was. Yet to her annoyance she found she did not reap the usual reward of her victories. Caroline, though defeated, was unsubdued. Before a week had passed, she was behaving more outrage-

ously than ever; and apparently unaware that she had
ever been to blame. During the first three or four years
no serious cause of quarrel arose between them. And for
the time being Lady Melbourne, followed by the rest
of her family, acted on her customary principle of
making the best of things. The Lambs treated Caroline
as a child, laughing at her vagaries when she was in a
good temper; when she was cross, ignoring them.
This was not, in her view, the way in which a heroine
had a right to be treated. She grew more discontented
than ever.

William did not annoy her in the same way. He at
least could be trusted to appreciate her. But even
William, she began to discover as time went on, was
not all she required. He was not distinguished enough
for one thing. The man of her choice must be admired
by all: William seemed quite happy to follow his tastes
unnoticed by anyone. Caroline heard people say that he
was never going to do anything; and influenced as she
always was by her company, she began to think they
must be right. This might not have mattered if he had
been completely satisfactory in his relation to her. But
he was not. The realist in him made him incapable of
playing up to her romantic conception of what a lover
should be. As early as 1807 we find her contrasting his
behaviour to her at a theatre unfavourably with that of

George, newly engaged to Lady Elizabeth Foster's daughter, Caroline. "I could not help remarking the difference between a husband and a lover!" she commented. "George had been an hour and a half at the play before William appeared." Once the honeymoon excitement was over, William's affection had settled down into a tranquil sunshiny sentiment in keeping with his personality. This was so unlike Caroline's idea of love that she began to doubt if he was in love at all.

Here she was wrong. But it was true that William was not ideally suited to her. In spite of all her faults, Caroline was not altogether to blame for the failure of her marriage. At nineteen years old the good in her was still partly uncorrupted by her egotism: and someone who understood how to foster its development, might have managed to make her a possible if not a perfect wife. But this needed a very special type of man, at once firm, tender and magnetic, prepared to guide her every step, and endowed with a moral majesty that could fire her hero-worship, while keeping her in healthy fear of his disapproval. Poor William! He was the last man to fill this role. Apart from anything else he was far too young. Love had inveigled him into matrimony before he was ready for it. He was still too preoccupied with forming his own tastes, and discovering his own point of view, to assume the responsibilities of a husband. But at no age would he have been the right husband for Caroline. For it was not in him to be an autocrat. The masterfulness he had shown on his honeymoon was the unique effect of an unprecedented burst of emotion. When this cooled, he relapsed into the man his temperament and Lady Melbourne had made him; passive, self-protective, indulgent, his first principle to let people alone, his first instinct to avoid trouble. Nor was he able to encourage Caroline's idealism. He did not believe in it. Attractive though they might be, at bottom he thought her high-flown fancies great nonsense; and he could not resist telling her so. His dark eyes agleam with mischief, he twitched aside, one by one, the veils of rose-coloured sentimentalism with which Devonshire House tried to cover the seamy side of life; exposed the weaknesses of the characters she had been brought up to revere; pointed out the fallacies involved in the religious and moral systems that commanded the respect of average mankind. Even his own relation to her was not protected from the disillusioning light of his realism. At the same time he assured her that he loved her, it amused him also to tell her that he had loved before, to recount the chronicles of earlier and less reputable amours. All this had its effect on Caroline. It did not make her cynical herself; this was too much against her nature. But it undermined the force of the few restraining principles of conduct implanted in her by native refinement and school-room education. If it was true—and William said it was—that everyone really did as they liked, and that it was silly to be shocked by them, there was clearly no reason why she should not do as she liked; and no one had the right to be shocked by her.

In these circumstances it was only a question of time when their marriage came to grief. During its first few years it was kept together by the ardour of their youthful passion. Even then they sometimes quarrelled; but they delighted so much in each other that they were always able to make it up. But as passion faded, a change came. The differences between them rose more and more to the surface, showing themselves in a continuous mutual irritation. They were always having rows. At first they tried to make them up in the old way:

"I think lately, my dear William," writes Caroline in 1809, "we have been very troublesome to each other; which I take wholesale to my own account and mean to correct, leaving you in retail a few little things which I know you will correct. . . . Condemn me not to silence and assist my imperfect memory. I will, on the other hand, be silent of a morning, entertaining after dinner; docile, fearless as a heroine in the last volume of her troubles, strong as a mountain tiger, and active as those young savages, Basil's boys."

It needed a harder heart than William's to resist so engaging an appeal as this: he responded to her overtures with a will. But it was no use. Caroline was a tiger all right, but not docile. However warm their reconciliations, they soon quarrelled again; more and more frequently and with growing bitterness; till gradually they abandoned the struggle to restore their marriage to its pristine harmony. Indeed the spirit needed to unite them was no longer there. Caroline went on saying she adored William: but, in fact, once her vanity was no longer involved in her love, once she had realized that William would never be able to play the part she had assigned him in her scheme of life, she ceased to care for him very much. He was more faithful. On him the Fairy Queen's spell could never lose its power. But he had grown equally disheartened about their marriage. If it were not Caroline's fault—and he hated to think it was—it must be a fault inherent in the nature of the relationship. He became profoundly disillusioned about marriage itself. In his Commonplace Book he noted down with caustic melancholy the conclusions forced on him by his experience of the matrimonial state:

"The general reason against marriage is this—that two minds, however congenial they may be, or however submissive the one may be to the other, can never act like one.

By taking a wife a man certainly adds to the list of those who have a right to interfere with and advise him, and he runs the risk of putting in his own way another very strong and perhaps insuperable obstacle to his acting according to his own opinions and inclinations.

By marrying you place yourself upon the defensive instead of the offensive in society, which latter is admitted to be in all contentions the most advantageous mode of proceeding.

Before marriage the shape, the figure, the complexion carry all before them; after marriage the mind and character unexpectedly claim their share, and that the largest, of importance.

Before I was married, whenever I saw the children and the dogs allowed, or rather caused, to be troublesome in any family, I used to lay it all to the fault of the master of it, who might at once put a stop to it if he pleased. Since I have married, I find that this was a very rash and premature judgment."

No—experience had proved his old philosophy of detachment only too true. His first attempt to leave his patch of neutrality had turned out as disastrous as he could have feared: trying to combine one's life with that of someone else ended inevitably in failure. Further he found that it had a deplorable effect on his character. Under the unprecedented strain imposed by the intimacy of married life, his naturally hot temper broke through the smooth surface under which he had, since childhood, managed to conceal it. Caroline began the rows; but, once his patience was exhausted, William raged even more violently than she did. Lack of control shocked his most sacred convictions: each time he lost his temper he apologized to her in horror-stricken remorse. But he began to find out that he could not restrain himself except by avoiding the occasion of anger; and that the only way to do this was to keep out of Caroline's way. By 1810 their relationship had insensibly slipped on to a new footing. They still had jokes in common, still wrote and talked to one another about books and politics. But they went their own ways; each had begun elsewhere than in the other to seek his chief satisfaction in life.

```
┌─────────────────────────────────┐
│                                 │
│          Chapter V              │
│                                 │
│        THE HOUSE OF             │
│         COMMONS                 │
│                                 │
└─────────────────────────────────┘
```

WILLIAM, like most men, turned for consolation to his work. Whether it was the sort of work best suited to him is doubtful. The speculative mind finds little opportunity to exercise itself in the humdrum mixture of compromise and practical business, which is parliamentary life. William was interested not in getting things done, but in discovering truth. Faced with a political problem, his mind sought instinctively less to solve it than to divine its causes: and thence to discern what light they cast on the general laws governing human affairs. Where others proposed a plan of action, he made a generalization. Further, English politics are party politics. And William recognized facts far too clearly to imagine that any single party could ever be wholly in the right. He might stick to a leader from loyalty or affection, but never with that blind conviction which makes party warfare a pleasure.

However, he had always made it his practice to fall in gracefully with whatever destiny circumstances indicated for him. It was universally accepted that the eldest son of a great family should go into the House of Commons; into the House of Commons, therefore, he went. As a matter of fact he did it with a very good will. If politics were not the best profession for him, they were far from being the worst. He had been brought up in the world of affairs; it came naturally to him to take a part in it. His chief interest, too, was human nature, and politics exhibited this on the most spectacular scale. Even if he had never taken an active part in them, they would always have formed a chief subject of his thought. Nor were they without their appeal to his imaginative side. He was acutely responsive to the romance of history in the making, to the drama of great events: and to national sentiment. Among the many contradictory elements of his complex nature lurked a strain of mystical patriotism. The thought of England—her great destiny, her majestic and immemorial past—sent a mysterious thrill of awe and veneration vibrating through the deepest fibres of his being.

He was further encouraged to like politics, by the privileged conditions in which he entered them. The society into which he was born might force eldest sons into public life: but in return it admitted them under special advantages. In those pre-democratic days, members of influential families had a prior claim on all the prizes of the profession. Even a stupid Whig magnate had a considerable place in his Party. One as clever as William was almost certain of achieving a commanding position at an early age. From the first, he was treated in a manner to make the mouths of ambitious young politicians of to-day water with envy. There was no need to make himself known. He had lived among the leaders of his Party since childhood. And as soon as he entered the House, they took him into their confidence, told him their private views; and, what was still more flattering, asked him his. Already in 1807 Lord Holland was writing to consult him about the choice of a leader: he was invited to informal councils at Holland House, where he would sit listening to Lord Grey and his host, as they discussed over the port, who should speak for the Opposition in a forthcoming debate. Altogether there was a great deal to please him in his profession. When in 1809 he began to throw his full energies into it, he did so without effort.

It was lucky he could. For the state of affairs that confronted him was not in itself one to inspire enthusiasm. During the first years of the nineteenth century, the Whig party was in a state of chaotic frustration. It was long indeed since it had stood for any active policy. Originally formed to support Parliament in its struggle with the King for ultimate sovereignty in the Constitution, it had achieved its essential object nearly a hundred years before, by expelling the Stuarts. During the long period of placid prosperity which followed, it had nothing to do but sit back and consolidate its victory. Now and again this involved a little work. Under the direction of Sir Robert Walpole, the Whigs established the Cabinet system: they also resisted the misguided efforts of George III to retrieve the lost powers of the Crown. But in the main they found themselves sufficiently occupied in drawing large sinecures, and extolling the principles of the glorious revolution of 1688. Nor was their inertia unpopular. The people of England were glad enough of a period unvexed by fundamental issues. But towards the end of the century a change came. The industrial revolution, by turning England from an agricultural to a manufacturing country, began to disturb that balance which must exist in any society between political and economic power. No longer were the land and its aristocratic owners the sole masters of the country's wealth. This position was shared by a new and rising class, part manufacturers, part workmen; who now demanded a voice in the government of the nation, proportionate to their economic influence. Nonconformists, free-traders, and of humble birth, they noted with irritation that the country was run in the interests of Protectionists, Anglicans and Lords. They clamoured for legal reform, fiscal reform, religious emancipation; above all they asked for that Parliamentary reform which, by destroying the aristocratic monopoly of seats, would readjust the balance of government in their favour. And they invoked all manner of novel and alarming doctrines, Equality, the Rights of Man, the Principle of Utility, to give moral justification to their claims. How far and in what manner these claims might be granted, by what means existing institutions could be modified in harmony with the new balance of power, were to be the problems that occupied the next forty years of English history.

Once more fundamental issues were raised. And the old parties had to decide which side they were going to take in the struggle. This was easy enough for the Tories. They had always approved of privilege, and disliked tradesmen. But the Whigs were more ambiguously placed. For, though in theory they considered themselves the upholders of progress and liberty, in fact they had a vested interest in the existing régime. Composed as they were largely of landed proprietors, they did not, any more than the Tories, like the idea of surrendering their power to a set of blackguardly commercials with Yorkshire accents and nonconformist consciences. A few exalted spirits among them threw in their lot with the cause of the future. The Duke of Norfolk drank to Our Sovereign the People; Mr. Whitbread took up Penal Reform; young Mr. Grey developed an interest in the representation question. But they were not enough to carry the party with them. It was to need the pressure of a powerful public opinion outside Parliament to drive the Whigs as a whole on to the Reform side. For the first thirty years of the century Whig opinion was bewildered, divided and wavering.

Anyway, before these new problems had come clearly to the front, before indeed the average M.P. had realized their existence, all forward movement was suddenly checked by two events abroad. First the French Revolution frightened the respectable people of every party to such a degree as to put them for the time being against any drastic changes: and then the Napoleonic War disposed them to shelve all domestic problems, till victory was won. At its beginning, some advanced Whigs had opposed the war; but by 1807 all the most influential were united to resist the common enemy. The natural outcome of such a situation should have been a Coalition between Whig and Tory. And after Pitt's death it was tried. But it collapsed within two years of William's entry into Parliament. The aged George III took the opportunity of one of his rare intervals of sanity to perform the last of his many acts of political folly. Obsessed by a confused idea that his right to the throne depended on the penal laws against Roman Catholics, he suddenly demanded that all his Ministers should pledge themselves not to bring in Catholic Emancipation. Catholic Emancipation was one of the few measures that all the Whigs were agreed in approving; the Whig Ministers therefore had to go out of office.

The effect of this combination of circumstances was to leave the Whigs in a parlous condition indeed. It was bad enough to find themselves indefinitely in opposition. But what made it far worse was that they could discover nothing they could agree to oppose. The chief question of the day was the war: and on this, most important Whigs sympathized with the Government. The problems of home affairs were in abeyance: in any case on every one of them, except the forbidden topic of Catholic Emancipation, they were at odds with one another. As long as Charles Fox was alive, people had been prepared to sink their differences out of loyalty to him. But after his death no one was left with sufficient personality to impose his will on the party. For the time being the Whigs were kept together only by their family and social

traditions. Though they disagreed on every political is-
sue, they continued all the same to marry one another's
daughters, to dine at Holland House and to spend their
leisure hours at Brooks's. These practices however, delightful though they might be, were not in themselves
enough to supply the want of a faith or a leader. Gradually party spirit weakened, party organization disintegrated; till by 1809 it had become such a smoky confusion
of shifting opinions, bickering factions, and competing
individuals, as to plunge the unfortunate historian, who
tries to disentangle it, into baffled despair.

Three groups dominated the general chaos: the Grenvillites, the Foxites, and the Mountain. Of these the
Grenvillites, composed of the powerful Grenville family
and their hangers-on, represented Whiggism in its strictly
dynastic aspect. They abhorred change as much as the
Tories; from whom they differed mainly in their conviction that only the great Whig families, and more
especially the Grenville family, had the right to govern
England. The Foxites, on the other hand, led by Lords
Holland and Grey, regarded themselves as the repository
of the pure milk of Whig doctrine. Academic, intran-
sigent, and tremendously aristocratic, they rejected all
proposals not in accordance with the principles of Charles
Fox; scorned economics; approved reform in theory, but
shrank from it in practice; and made it a matter of con-

science not to work with anyone with whom they disagreed about anything. The Mountain was a more
heterogeneous body, made up, partly of lively young pa-
tricians with a taste for advanced ideas, and partly of
clever members of the middle class, brought into Parliament by noble patrons. They were openly against the
war, vociferously in favour of any kind of reform; such
vigour as remained in the party resided in them.

Around these main groups hovered a motley mob of
smaller combinations and isolated personalities. All sec-
tions quarrelled with each other, and among themselves.
Some were for the Whigs taking a strong line, some for
their retiring from Parliament altogether, some for their
coming to terms with the Tories. Connections were all
the time crumbling and reshaping themselves; all the
time, ambitious men flitted from one group to another,
according as each seemed more likely to retrieve the fortunes of the Party. The Whig lobbies buzzed with a
continual rumour of baseless hopes and abortive intrigues.
By the time William was ready to turn his full attention to his party, it presented a deplorable spectacle; an
army in rout, without order, purpose or morale.

He approached it in a detached spirit. Long before he
entered the House of Commons, he had begun to out-
grow his youthful idealism. And by now his attitude to
politics had matured, to be of a piece with his attitude to

everything else; sceptical, realistic, cautious. Natural prudence was intensified by the age in which he lived. It is very difficult for us, hardened as we are by the daily spectacle of catastrophies far more appalling, to realize the extraordinary shock given to our forefathers by the French Revolution. Just across the Channel they saw what seemed at first to be no more than a mild constitutional movement change within four years to a bloody terror, in which people just like themselves, whom they had dined with on their visits abroad, were stripped destitute of all their possessions, and often horribly murdered. These events undermined their root confidence in the stability of civilization. If such things happened in France, why not in England? The idea that they might, began to obsess them.

To such an obsession William was peculiarly susceptible. Detached hedonism is not less dependent on material circumstance than other human philosophies. Its sunny suavity, its easy broadmindedness, can flourish only in security. During mortal conflicts people inevitably grow morose and partisan. Once he had come to years of political discretion, William saw only too clearly that revolution would mean the end of all that made his life worth living, the destruction of the foundation on which his precariously adjusted peace of mind was built. Fear of popular violence loomed ever at the back of his consciousness. It was the single thing that was able to throw his poised judgment off its balance: throughout his life it was a determining motive in his political views. Yet it did not drive him into blind reaction. Belief in liberty, in toleration, was the very fibre of his thought. Moreover, his vigorous understanding had combined with his Glasgow education, to make him a man of his time. He realized that the world he lived in was changing, and that there was no use in trying to stop it. Poised between two extremes, his point of view was necessarily impartial. And this impartiality was increased both by his intellectual self-confidence and by his lack of ambition. He did not particularly want to get on; he did not care if others agreed with him. And he had no interest in politics except in so far as he was able to speak his honest opinion about them. Thus, disinterested and unenthusiastic, inquisitive and unprejudiced, the corners of his mouth turned down in ironic amusement, he stepped on to the political stage.

One wonders what the other actors thought of him. For he differed strikingly from the ordinary member. William, like most philosophical persons, was not naturally an orator. He was too self-critical to be able to let himself go in public. Stammering and colloquial, as if he were thinking aloud, his words would trickle forth; wandering away into generalization, or pausing as with fastidiousness he sought out the phrase that might most precisely express his shade of meaning. Moreover, the line he took was generally so unexpected, as to make it difficult to know precisely where his political sympathies lay. "I know he will be reckoned too scrupulous and conscientious for a good Party man," said Lady Bessborough, "but I cannot help admiring the firm integrity of his character." This was a friendly way of putting it. To those less personally prejudiced in his favour, William's conduct, during his first few years in Parliament, might well have seemed a mere exhibition of caprice. At one time we find him refusing to back his Party in their attack on Lord Ellenborough's position in the Ministry; on another, voting in favour of the advanced Sir Samuel Romilly's proposals on Penal Reform. He was strongly against the Government over Catholic Emancipation, strongly on their side about the war. When the Duke of York was assailed by the extreme Whigs for selling commissions in the Army through the convenient agency of his mistress, Mary Ann Clarke, William followed them. But not, he was careful to say, because he was certain of the Duke's guilt, but for reasons of public policy. And two years later he voted for the Duke's reinstatement.

He kept a journal of his early Parliamentary impressions. And this also reveals a contradictory spirit. He seems to take an impish pleasure in discovering the disillusioning paradoxes of public life: the harm done by good intentions, the weaknesses of revered institutions. It amused him to note that Napoleon, one of the worst men in the world, made his subjects happier than most virtuous rulers; that human beings, so it appeared from the Peninsular War, seemed more likely to get what they wanted by behaving violently than by being reasonable. Nor could he feel much respect for the wisdom of the Sovereign People. "It is impossible not to laugh," he said, "at their blunders, ignorance and fury; at the same time it is impossible not to be struck with the most serious alarm upon the subject."

None the less, his opinions were not so negative, nor his actions so capricious, as appearances might suggest. Coming fresh to the game, it was inevitable that he should roam inquisitively around from one set of views to another; getting a sort of wilful enjoyment from finding out the faults of each. But as he lived, he learned. Bit by bit, a store of experience accumulated itself in his mind; and on the strength of it his own political ideas began to take shape. They were not those of the Party to which he was officially attached. His detached mind was unlikely to be impressed by the welter of squabble and wobble, in which the Whigs floundered. William thought them factious. "The fault of opposition," he remarked, "is a determination to make differences where few exist;

and those trifling." Nor, in point of fact, did he agree with any of the main groups of Whig opinion. The Grenvillites had nothing to offer a man who liked ideas; for they had none. The Foxites, on the other hand, bristled with them. But theirs were obsolete. Of what interest was it to William to preserve the purity of a creed formulated forty years before? As for the Mountain, they were the worst of the lot; against the war, and in favour of all sorts of risky changes. He could agree with the Tories sooner than with them. Yet he was against the Tories too. Their views were out of date, and they themselves stupid. William was still young enough to have a horror of being thought stupid.

As usual, he found himself adopting a middle course. He wanted a policy moderate and rational; that faced modern problems, but involved no threat to that aristocratic supremacy on which in his view the security of civilization depended. He soon found he was not alone. Similar thoughts had been circulating among a number of young men from both parties, headed, ironically enough, by that peculiar object of William's youthful contempt, Canning. Canning is an ambiguous personality. Few people liked him in his lifetime; nor is it possible to feel enthusiastic about him to-day. There is something indefinably charlatanish about the impression he makes, with his flashy eloquence, his restless intriguing

ambition, his sharp, arrogant, egotistic face. Yet, as is so
often the case in this mysterious world, he was more
genuinely creative than many sincerer persons. It was
he who, first among English statesmen of the nineteenth
century, offered conservative-minded people a constructive
political creed. Himself, he was against Parliamentary
reform. England in his view did very well under an
aristocracy. Besides, he thought the whole democratic
philosophy great nonsense. "It is the business of the legis-
lature," he once said, "to remedy practical grievances, not
to run after theoretical perfection." On the other hand
he thought some of the practical measures demanded by
the reforming parties reasonable. He was all for legal
reform, and emancipation, and considered that many
people had taken up Democracy, because they thought
it the only means of getting these measures through.
And the way to prevent this, in his opinion, was to show
that the old system could be made to do the same work
equally well. "Those who resist improvements as inno-
vations," so he put it, "will soon have to accept innova-
tions that are not improvements."

Such were the ideas that he propounded over the dinner table, or in conversation with his fellow members as
they walked home from the House in the early hours of
the morning. And he presented them in a sparkling up-
to-date style, nicely calculated to take the fancy of the

bright young spirits of the day. What a comfort to find that one could be anti-revolutionary without appearing stodgy or old-fashioned! It was no wonder that he soon had a troop of followers. Two of them, Ward and Huskisson, were already well-acquainted with William. Ward was one of his regular boon companions, a handsome young aristocrat, all brilliance and sensibility, and the height of fashion. Huskisson was a relation by marriage. As such he had never appealed to William. Earnest, middle class, and with an unfortunate habit of falling down on the most embarrassing occasions, he was the sort of man whom the Lambs thought a great joke. But he had a massive, well-trained mind and an extraordinary knowledge of finance; and when William saw him at work in Parliament he began to conceive a great respect for him. With such connections, William was quickly admitted into the inner circle of the Canningites. Once there he was captivated.

For their part the Canningites were only too pleased to have him. In spite of his youthful contradictiousness, and his halting way of speaking, William's reputation had steadily grown throughout his time in Parliament. Indeed, his speeches were better worth listening to than those of many more accomplished orators. They were continually lit up by flashes of insight, pungent turns of wit. Besides, everybody liked him so much. As at Cambridge and the Bar, people were delighted to work with anyone so good-natured, so intelligent, so patently innocent of any desire to push himself. "I hardly know anyone," says Ward affectionately, "of whom everybody entertains so favourable an opinion." And the barometer of fame at Holland House told the same tale. "William Lamb," writes Lady Holland, "is certainly one of the most rising men in public."

Yet his situation was not so comfortable as it looked. Once more his circumstances impeded the true development of his talents. If he really agreed with Canning, he should have thrown in his lot with him wholeheartedly; openly joined him, devoted his every effort to forwarding his cause. But this meant difficulties. Canning was officially a Tory. For one brought up in the inner circle of Whig society, it was an extremely unpleasant step to put himself publicly under Tory leadership. Every prejudice of William's home, of the houses he visited, of the clubs where he spent his mornings, was against it. Further, though he might think poorly of the Whigs as politicians, personally they were his greatest friends. To leave them, when they were so obviously in a bad way, seemed an odious disloyalty. It would have been easy only to someone with a passionate conviction in the rightness of his cause. William's upbringing had been such as to make him question every conviction. His sense of personal obligation, on the other hand, was peculiarly strong. In a world of illusion, individual affections, and the loyalties consequent on them, alone seemed solid. Leaving the Whigs was simply one of the things William felt he could not do. He therefore took a temporizing line. In public he never supported his party against Canning; in private he pressed his claims. But he called himself a Whig; and when early in 1812 the Prime Minister, anxious to strengthen his administration by the infusion of young blood, offered William a post in the administration, he refused.

With an agitated ingenuity he tried to persuade himself that he was fulfilling a moral duty. He could do more good where he was; changing one's party set a demoralizing example to others; it was subversive of the very principles of loyalty. In the ardour of self-defence he even went so far as to say that a man was only justified in doing it, if he thought that otherwise he would go to Hell. But no amount of argument could alter the fact that William was in a thoroughly false position. All he could do was to wait; uncertainly hoping for some sudden change in the political situation, by which it might be possible for a coalition of moderate men of both sides, led by Canning, to come into power.

In the spring of 1812 there was a chance that this might occur. The Government had been doing so badly that it looked as if they would not be able to go on much longer. Political London was in a hubbub of excitement; George III had gone mad again, and anything might happen. In the lobbies of the Houses of Parliament, in the drawing-rooms of great houses, people arrived every moment, bursting with new rumours. Canningite hopes grew high. Alas, they were to be disappointed. In the wavering balance of competing factions, the deciding factor was the line taken by the Prince Regent. Since he had always called himself a Whig, the Canningites imagined that he would look with favour on a more liberal administration. This only showed that they did not know the Prince Regent. He did ask Lord Wellesley to form a Coalition; but after days of hovering and intrigue, in which the Prince tearfully reiterated his unalterable fidelity to his old friends, he threw them over in favour of their opponents. This turned the scale. On 19th March, 1812, a petition was brought forward in the House of Lords asking for an all-party Government. Late in the evening, amid the gilt and candlelight of Melbourne House, Lady Melbourne and a crowd of Whig ladies waited anxiously to hear the result. At last, long after midnight, William and his friends trailed in, glum and crestfallen; the petition had been decisively defeated. This defeat was confirmed a month or two later in the House of Commons. The extreme Tories were safe for ten years more. The hopes of the Canningites were indefinitely postponed.

This set-back to his friends need not have been a check to William's own career. His reputation was now so high that the Prince of Wales wrote himself in the most pressing way, to offer him a place in the Cabinet. But William felt he could not accept it. The failure of Canning had hit him particularly hard. For it meant that he felt himself condemned to a false position for ever. Since he disagreed with his own party, but yet could not bring himself to leave it, all his hopes had been pinned on the chance of Coalition. Now that this proved impossible, there seemed no place for him in politics. A deep discouragement spread over his spirit; which swelled into a wider disillusionment with public life as a whole. Surveying his Parliamentary career in the clear sunless light of his present disappointment, he wondered if he was not essentially unsuited to the career of statesman. He could not speak as he wished in the House, he could not even think there. The ideas which stirred in him at home, found there no channel for expression. His profession had turned out as great a disappointment as his marriage:

"Sir Edward Coke says, somewhere or another," he noted in his journal, "that he is certain that God enlarges and enlightens the understanding of men when

138

they are sitting in Courts of Justice. Such is the difference between a man who by his habits and feelings is formed for public affairs, and one who is unfitted for them. The former finds himself encouraged, invigorated, and strengthened by the consciousness that he is acting upon the spur of the occasion before the eyes of men, subject to their censure in his failure, but sure to reap their approbation by his success. All these circumstances oppress and overwhelm the latter, and deprive him of the use of those powers which perhaps he possesses in an eminent degree. By this (Sir E. Coke's saying) we must, of course understand that he found in that situation his own mental perceptions more quick and clear, and his judgment more settled and distinct, than upon other occasions. For myself, I must own the House of Commons has upon me quite a different effect. I can walk in the shrubbery here at Brocket Hall and reason and enlarge upon almost any topic; but in the House of Commons, whether it be from apprehension, or heat, or long waiting, or the tediousness of much of what I hear, a torpor of all my faculties almost always comes upon me, and I feel as if I had neither ideas nor opinions, even upon the subjects which interest me the most deeply."

And now more sordid cares arose to complete his discouragement with his profession. £2,000 a year was not much on which to keep up the position of a man of fashion and a member of Parliament; especially for the husband of Caroline. The young Lambs consistently over-spent themselves. If there was a General Election—elections in those pre-Reform days cost anything up to £50,-000—William did not see what he was going to do. He was resolved not to go to his parents for money. What with Lady Melbourne's parties, Lord Melbourne's card debts, and the joyous expenses of their children, the family income was nothing like as big as it had been. From every point of view, William's immediate political prospects looked black. When in July, 1812, the Government did declare for an election, William reluctantly decided not to stand. Lady Melbourne, deeply distressed at this set-back to her ambitions for him, besought him to reconsider his position, and offered him all the money he would want. But it was one of the occasions when she found herself up against a force in him that she could not move. In August, William was, for the first time for fourteen years, a man of leisure.

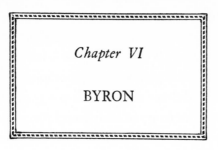

Chapter VI

BYRON

A S A MATTER of fact, if he had stayed in politics, he would have found it hard to give his mind to them. Since 1809 the disturbing elements in his married life had steadily intensified, till now in 1812 they had burst out in a storm that was deafening London. While William was hobnobbing with the Canningites, Caroline had also found new interests. Since the role of wife had proved an inadequate vehicle for her dreams, she turned to other fields. Her first activities were social; it might be pleasant to be the centre of an intellectual circle. She never had any difficulty in attracting people, when she wanted to. Within a short time she was the friend of most of those men of letters who were sufficiently presentable socially to have achieved the entrance to the best houses. Rogers, Monk Lewis, Tom Moore, any or all of them might be found of an afternoon in her sitting-room, reading aloud their works to her while she sketched their portraits. She also made some new female friends. These were of a less desirable kind. Partly in order to annoy her relations-in-law, partly from a desire to impress the world by her emancipation of mind, she struck up with two of the few women of position who had contrived to put themselves outside the lax limits of Whig convention, Lady Wellesley and Lady Oxford. Neither can have been very attractive in herself, to one brought up at Devonshire House. Lady Wellesley was a Frenchwoman of very shady reputation, who had borne her husband several children before she married him; Lady Oxford, a tarnished siren of uncertain age, who pursued a life of promiscuous amours on the fringes of society, in an atmosphere of tawdry eroticism and tawdrier culture. Reclining on a sofa, with ringlets disposed about her neck in seductive disarray, she would rhapsodize to her lovers on the beauties of Pindar and the hypocrisy of the world. Caroline laughed at her affectations: her aristocratic eye also noted that Lady Oxford was a trifle common. But there was something in Caroline that responded to her luscious sentimentalizings. It was undeniably agreeable to a person of sensibility to receive

142

a letter beginning, "Let us, my sweetest friend, improve the passing hour and with its help turn to the contemplation of true wisdom. . . . We will defy the censorious"; or inviting her opinion as to whether learning Greek purified or inflamed the passions. "Caroline seems to have more faith in theory than in practice," remarked her caustic cousin Harriet, "to judge, at least, by those she consults on these nice points of morality."

Indeed, her new friends did not please her relations. William himself implored her not to risk her good name by mixing in such worthless company; Lady Bessborough was distressed; and Lady Melbourne perfectly furious. Whatever the failings of her own friends, they had always been delightful, interesting people, and duchesses as well. "As you love singularity," she wrote to Caroline, "it may be some satisfaction to you to know you are the only woman who has any pretensions to character who ever courted Lady Wellesley's acquaintance, that I never saw anyone sup in her party. . . . A married woman should consider that by such laxity she not only compromises her own honour and character but also that of her husband—but you seek only to please yourself."

Nor, as Lady Melbourne had already discovered, was having supper with Lady Wellesley the worst of Caroline's indiscretions. Social success did not satisfy her ambitions. A heroine's life, as she conceived it, included drama as well as admiration; and drama to Caroline meant love affairs. In 1810 her name began to be mentioned in connection with Lady Holland's son by her first marriage, Sir Godfrey Webster. Personally he had even less to recommend him than Lady Oxford; a coarse, handsome young rake, whose chief boast it was that he never went to bed till nine in the morning, and whose sporting reputation was so dingy, that even the Whips Club—a very easy-going body—would have nothing to do with him. Caroline, however, chose to regard him as a fine example of dashing manliness, unpopular only on account of his admirable contempt for vulgar opinion. Looked at in such a light, he made an adequate, if not an ideal hero for her purposes. She flung herself into a violent flirtation with him, which she took care to make as public as possible. They went everywhere together. Ward, calling one afternoon at Melbourne House to see William, was surprised to find himself taken up to Lady Caroline's room; where, pacing the floor in theatrical agitation, she poured forth the story of her unfortunate passion.

It was not surprising that she soon had Lady Bessborough and Lady Melbourne on her track again, this time reinforced by Lady Holland. As usual, when faced with disapproval, Caroline lost her nerve. She deluged Lady Holland with a flood of incoherent and unpunctuated letters, in which she alternately denied with scorn, and penitently admitted, that there was anything between her and Sir Godfrey. Lady Holland was not impressed. However, she told Caroline she was willing to believe that the whole thing was a pretence, worked up to attract attention. These were not at all the sort of grounds on which Caroline wished to be acquitted. Lady Holland's words, so she picturesquely expressed it, lay "like a weight on her stomach," and she performed the most prodigious feats of intellectual contortionism, in her efforts to prove that she was at the same time a blameless and adoring wife to William and the victim of an irresistible infatuation for Sir Godfrey.

Lady Holland remained sceptical; Caroline then lost her temper. "As to the gnats and mites that dare to peck at me," she fulminated, "let them look to themselves. If I choose, you shall see them lick the dust I tread on. Lady Holland, if this is the case, I shall be courted by you. . . . I remain more sincerely than you deserve, Caroline Lamb."

To Lady Melbourne she defended herself by saying that the whole thing was William's fault: his cynicism had destroyed her moral sense. This was the last excuse likely to mollify Lady Melbourne, already seething with indignation on William's behalf. They continued to wrangle till May, when Lady Melbourne got a letter from

Caroline saying all was at an end. She had been sitting in her morning-room—so ran her story—with her child, "on the brink of perdition," when suddenly her dog, a present from Sir Godfrey, snapped at the baby and shortly afterwards fell down foaming at the mouth. It flashed upon her that as a judgment for her sins it had gone mad and was going to bite the baby. So dreadful an idea brought her to her senses. Tearing from her arm a bracelet made of Sir Godfrey's hair, she rushed to her writing-table and wrote off to William, confessing all and imploring forgiveness. Whether there was a word of truth in this sensational piece of autobiography, it is impossible to say. Certainly, if there was, it produced a less decisive effect than might have been anticipated. The flirtation lingered on until the end of the summer, and then it was Sir Godfrey who called it off. Caroline seems to have taken his defection with unexpected calm. Her mood had changed: she was absorbed in social life, in reading, in the new dance, the Waltz. Its pulsing lilt was exquisitely in tune with her spirit: and during the early part of 1812 she might have been found any morning along with the rest of the smart set of the period, the gentlemen in swathed neckcloths, the ladies in their filmy, high-waisted dresses, practising her steps in the painted ballroom of Melbourne House, to the sprightly strains of Ach du lieber Augustin. In the intoxication of these whirling delights, Sir Godfrey and his virile charms were forgotten.

But her passage with him had left a mark on her life that no amount of forgetfulness on her part could efface. Her reputation was seriously damaged by her choice of a lover, and still more by the way she had advertised her relationship with him. She had overstepped, as Lady Melbourne for instance had never done, the subtle line which separates what society condemned from what it condoned. From this time she could no longer afford to take any risk with her good name. More serious, she had widened the gulf between herself and William. William does not seem to have been jealous; he knew her well enough by this time to realize, like Lady Holland, that the whole thing was most likely a pretence and would soon pass. But even if her actual infidelity was fictitious, his sensitive spirit was deeply wounded to discover that she now had so little regard for his feelings as to be willing to flaunt it publicly. Once—it was at a ball on the evening of 11th July—his pent-up emotions broke forth. Caroline would not go home: and as William was turning to leave alone, he reminded her that it was the anniversary of their wedding day, passionately he called to her the thousand vows of constancy she had then made—now to all appearances utterly forgotten. For the moment Caroline was unmoved; but driving home by herself in

the grey light of the summer dawn, her naturally generous heart was overcome by an agonizing wave of self-
reproach; lying sleepless on her bed, she resolved to reform. She was sincere—only she could not keep it up.
Within a few days William watched her behaving as
impossibly as ever. And though even now he could not
help loving her, for the first time a strain of hard bitterness began to enter his disillusioned heart.

It was to grow stronger during the years that followed.
The Webster episode was only the rehearsal of a far
more distressing exhibition. In March, 1812, the first
part of *Childe Harold* was published to the world. Its
success was instantaneous and colossal. The sweep of its
rhetoric, its full-blooded romantic pessimism, its glowing
Turneresque landscapes, all torrents and ruins, and
patches of picturesque foreign colour, alike hit the taste
of the time. And so still more did the personality behind them; the figure of the author who, melancholy,
detached and scornful, his heart turned to marble by a
career of sin and sightseeing in every part of Europe,
stood out in melodramatic silhouette against the sublim-
ities of nature and the wreckage of empires. Besides, he
was a lord, and, it was rumoured, as beautiful as an angel:
such a lion had not appeared in London within living
memory. His book became the fashion as no poem ever
has before or since. Listening at the dinner table one

heard the words "Childe Harold" coming from every mouth; in St. James's Street, where its author lived, the traffic was held up by the press of carriages bearing notes of invitation for him; before a month had passed, the doors of every modish house in the capital had been flung open to announce—"Lord Byron."

On an unprejudiced observer he must have made an unexpected impression. There limped into the room a self-conscious youth, with a handsome sulky head, fidgety movements, showy, ill-fitting clothes, and a manner conspicuously lacking in the ease and naturalness usual in a man of his rank. Indeed, Byron at twenty-four was, in almost every respect, the opposite of the version of himself he sought to impose on the world. No one could have been less detached. By nature acutely sensitive to the opinion of others, his confidence had been early undermined by his lame leg, his bullying, drunken mother, and the poverty-stricken and provincial circumstances of his childhood. A gnawing, resentful mistrust of all men, and more especially of all women, warred continuously in his breast with an obsessing desire to make an impression on anyone by any means. There was nothing he would not do to score a hit or avoid a humiliation. Nor was he at heart a romantic. Fundamentally, Byron had a robust eighteenth-century mocking kind of outlook. But the romantic attitude, by the scope it gave for individual self-glorification, gratified his egotism: and he could not resist adopting it. His sophistication was equally false; a mask assumed to hide a torturing shyness. He trembled every time he had to enter a drawing-room; his conversation was that of a clever undergraduate, all impish brilliance, and wilful moods, and naïve affectations: and if he failed to please, he flung off in a pet. So far from being the experienced and disillusioned Childe Harold, he was a raw, nerve-ridden boy of genius, whose divine fire gleamed fitfully forth through an undignified turmoil of suspicion and awkwardness, theatrical pose and crude vanity.

Such was the real Byron. But the hostesses of London saw him as Childe Harold. And none more than Caroline. As might have been expected, she caught the Byron fever in a particularly virulent form. "I must meet him —I am dying to meet him," she told Rogers. "He has a club foot and bites his nails," Rogers replied. "If he is as ugly as Aesop," she insisted, "I must see him." A few days later her wish was gratified at a ball. Caroline staged the meeting with her usual sense of the theatre. When Byron was led up to her to be introduced, she gazed for a moment intently into his face, and then silently turned on her heel. That night she wrote in her diary, "Bad, mad and dangerous to know." This was equivalent to saying she had determined to know him very well. They met again two days later during an afternoon call at Holland House. This time as he was presented, Byron, thoroughly piqued by her behaviour at their first interview, began straight away: "This offer was made to you the other day. May I ask why you declined it?" History does not record her reply; but before they parted he had promised to come and see her. The affair between them was launched on its tumultuous course.

The events of this celebrated serio-comedy, as Byron called it, have been told and re-told, analysed and argued about, in a hundred different books. Yet much about it remains obscure. For the chief evidence on the subject is that of Caroline and Byron themselves: and they were both such confirmed liars, both so bent at all costs on making out a good case for themselves, that it is impossible to trust a word that either says. Further, their behaviour was so abnormally capricious as to make it hard, even when the facts are unquestioned, to divine their import. In Caroline, contradictory moods and different dramatic poses succeeded one another with the eye-deceiving rapidity of a quick-change act. While Byron was blown from his course at every turn, now by weakness, now by vanity.

However, from the welter of conflicting statements and inconsistent actions, one fact emerges. Neither was, in

any true sense, in love. Caroline of course thought she
was—more than anyone had ever been in love before.
And it is true that her emotions were violently agitated.
But it was not Byron she cared for: it was his reputation,
and still more the idea of herself in love with him. Beautiful, brilliant, seared with the flames of exotic passion,
and the most lionized man in England, he was everything she had all her life been seeking. Here at last was
a hero worthy of such a heroine. Firmly shutting her
eyes to everything but her own visions, she made up her
mind that she had found the love of her life. Byron was
less self-deceived. He knew quite well he was not in love.
Caroline was everything he liked least in women, stormy,
clever, and unfashionably thin; "I am haunted by a skele-
ton," he once remarked. But he had not the strength to
withstand her; and he never could refuse the chance of
a conquest. Moreover, young as he was, and dazzled by
the new and glittering world into which his fame had
so suddenly flung him, the prospect of an amour with one
of its reigning queens flattered him in a way he was
unable to resist. Once entangled, he played his part with
all the spirit he could muster. Society was presented
with the extraordinary spectacle of a love drama, performed in the most flamboyant, romantic manner by two
raging egotists, each of whom was in fact wholly absorbed in self.

They did not do it very well. Caroline over-acted her part, and Byron could not keep his up. Under the glaring spotlight of the public attention, they postured about the stage, getting in each other's way, tripping each other up, turning on one another in childish abuse, pausing to explain to the audience how abominably the other was behaving. Indeed, it would have been an ignominious exhibition enough, but for the personalities of the performers. But both in their varying degrees were people of genius: and in the most ludicrous postures, the most farcical contretemps, they managed somehow to remain magnetic and picturesque. Byron's most flagrant disloyalties sparkle with infectious humor: Caroline's wildest insincerity throbs with an eloquence that brings tears to the eyes. It is this ironic contrast between the glamour of its characters and the unseemly absurdity of the situations in which they were involved, that gives their story its peculiar piquancy to an amateur of the human comedy.

Caroline took the initiative, at once striking the high romantic note on which she intended the relationship to be conducted. "That beautiful pale face will be my fate," she noted, some time during the first week or so of their acquaintance. And she proceeded with a magnificent gesture of generosity to offer Byron all her jewels to sell, if he were hard up. He replied by sending her a rose accompanied by a note, couched in the best Childe Harold strain of insolent allurement: "Your Ladyship, I am told," it ran, "likes all that is new and rare—for a moment." This was only following her lead; how far he had decided to go, in these early days, is uncertain. However, any lingering hesitations he may have felt were soon dispelled by Lady Bessborough. She, fearing a repetition of the Webster affair, tried to discourage Byron by telling him that Caroline's infatuation was only assumed to pique another admirer. This roused all Byron's latent competitiveness: he determined not to rest till he was the acknowledged master of Caroline's heart.

From this time the affair rushed onwards in a gathering crescendo. Byron spent the greater part of every day in Caroline's room at Melbourne House; during the rare moments they were apart they communicated by means of letters and verses. Whether they ever became lovers in the fullest sense of the term is one of the unsolved problems of the whole mysterious business. Rogers, who knew them both well, denied it: and his denial is made more probable by the fact that Caroline was of that cerebral temperament, to which the pleasures of the imagination always mean more than the pleasures of the senses. On the other hand it is almost incredible that Byron should have been satisfied without this most practical proof of her subjugation. Whatever the truth may be, it is certain that some time in the summer they went

LADY CAROLINE LAMB in page's costume
From a miniature in the possession of Sir John Murray

through an odd mock marriage ceremony, exchanging rings and writing mutual vows in a book which they signed Byron and Caroline Byron.

Indeed, every stage of their passionate pilgrimage was marked by some theatrical gesture. Caroline was chiefly concerned to parade her tremendous conquest before the world. Throughout all the brilliant crowding activities of the London season, between the red festooned curtains of an opera box, amid the diadems and bare shoulders of a ball, driving round the park in the level evening sunshine, the lowering dark head and the ecstatic blonde one were conspicuous, side by side. They left every party together in Byron's carriage; if by chance only he was invited, Caroline would hang about outside among the link-boys to greet him with demonstrative ardour when he came out. She also created scandal by appearing at unexpected moments in his rooms, imperfectly disguised as a page, in a plumed hat, silver-laced jacket and tight scarlet pantaloons. He, for his part, ran through all the gamut of the Byronic attitudes: was by turns enigmatic, passionate, mocking and tragic. Sitting in her room, he would declaim with melodramatic desolation on the un-paralled iniquity of his own character; compared with him, he cried, William Lamb was as Hyperion to a satyr. On other occasions, with eyes lurid with jealousy, he would require Caroline to swear that she loved him better than William. And when she hesitated, "My God, you shall pay for this," he thundered. "I'll wring that little obstinate heart." He even made her give up waltzing on the ground that he could not bear to see her in the arms of another man. Caroline was jealous, too, and showed it in an even more spectacular fashion. Little Lord John Russell, at dinner at Spencer House, was startled to notice that Lady Caroline Lamb, seized by a fit of uncontrollable agitation, had bitten through the glass that she held in her hand; following her gaze across the table, he saw Lord Byron bending attentively over a beautiful woman next him.

Certainly the course of their love was the reverse of smooth. Rogers used often to arrive home in the afternoon to find the pair pacing his garden: they had quarrelled all day and wanted him to reconcile them. To Caroline, suffering had its compensations: existence was for the first time as exciting as she had always desired it. But Byron felt differently. At heart he liked life to move calmly and sensibly. It was only his desire to conquer Caroline that had made him play up to her heroics. Once his victory was won, he grew bored. Besides, he had an uncomfortable feeling that all this sensational exhibitionism made him look ridiculous. He grew more and more restive; by July he was longing to be quit of the whole affair.

Now, a new and powerful influence arose to encourage his longing. Byron had not taken to Lady Melbourne when he first met her. He only liked those who liked him: and Caroline's mother-in-law, he suspected, must be his enemy. As a matter of fact, Lady Melbourne was not ill-disposed towards Byron. Caroline's troubles, she had long ago made up her mind, were always Caroline's fault. On this occasion had she simply flung herself un-asked at a young man's head. And, according to Lady Melbourne's code, a young man was perfectly justified in making love to a married woman if she showed herself willing. In himself, Byron struck Lady Melbourne as extremely agreeable; she therefore made herself as pleas-ant to him as she could. Her success was immediate. Mistress as she was of the art of pleasing men, she made him feel more at ease than he had since his entry into London society. Moreover, he had a great deal in com-mon with her—much more than with Caroline. Her worldly wisdom, her caustic agreeability, and her equable temper, alike appealed to him; so for the matter of that did her cynicism and her lack of refinement. The Mel-bourne atmosphere was far more to Byron's taste than the Devonshire. After the delicacies and exaltations of an interview with Caroline, what a relief it was, what an indescribable relief, to turn into Lady Melbourne's rooms on the ground floor; where one could be as outspoken and flippant and disloyal as one liked, with no risk of being thought unkind or ungentlemanly. Besides, Lady Melbourne was so helpful: on her sofa she would sit, advising one in the most terse and entertaining way about how to manage a woman or how to save one's income. "The best friend I ever had in my life," he was to write later, "and the cleverest of women. If she had been a few years younger, what a fool she would have made of me had she thought it worth her while."

Lady Melbourne enjoyed his company as much as he did hers. At sixty-two it was gratifying indeed to be the favourite companion of the most sought-after young man in London—especially when it involved stealing him from Caroline. Nor had she so far outgrown her youth, as to be insensible to his attractions. It would be misleading to say that she was in love with him. Her friendship with Byron was at most an agreeable diversion from the serious business of her ambition. But she felt sufficiently warm towards him to acquire a strong bias in his favour. No doubt he was selfish and fickle—most men were in her experience. But he was sensible enough at bottom, as far as she could see. Discreetly managed, he should give no trouble.

Here she was wrong. The wild fire of genius that burned unsteadily in Byron's bosom made him at once more formidable and more unstable than she realized.

But she can hardly be blamed for her mistake. Possessed as he was by the wish to make a good impression, Byron was incapable of showing himself with complete honesty to anyone. And he had achieved an extraordinary dexterity at guessing the version of his character best calculated to win over the person he happened to be talking to. The Childe Harold pose he saw would be no good with Lady Melbourne; if she believed in it, she would not like it. Laughingly, therefore, and with an artful frankness, he represented himself as a straightforward, sensual male, weak, a trifle mischievous, and with no high-flown ideals about him, but essentially good-natured; the victim, not the master of others; anxious only for a quiet life and a little fun. It was not quite the truth. But it was close enough to it to be irresistibly convincing. Lady Melbourne was convinced. However, she did not lose her head. Her demeanour towards Byron was a masterpiece in the delicate art of friendship between older woman and younger man; easy, intimate and with a pleasant touch of flirtation about it, but never so ardent or so familiar as to be unsuitable to her age and position. She received his declarations of admiration with a teasing, flattering irony exactly calculated to keep the relationship between them at that comfortable temperature which would make it firm.

"You say, 'I admire you certainly as much as ever you

were admired,'" she says on one occasion, "and a great deal more I assure you than ever I was. I have been beloved—but Love is not admiration. Lovers admire, of course, without knowing why. Yours therefore is much more flattering as I sd. the other day—but you quite astonished me when I found your usual playfulness chang'd into such a formal tirade. I have hardly yet recover'd my surprise—now I have told you everything & have shown myself truly to you; I can not see why you should wish that you had not known me. It can not lead to any regret and if circumstances should not stop it entirely our Friendship will be very pleasant to both as any sentiment must be where all is sunshine—and where love does not introduce itself, there can be no jealousys, torments & quarrels. . . . Once you told me you did not understand Friendship. I told you I would teach it you, & so I will, if you do not allow C. to take you quite away."

In reality it was she who was taking him away from C. She made use of the friendship to engineer a break. Far too intelligent to take a solemn line about the matter, she constituted herself Byron's confidante; listened sympathetically to his complaints of Caroline's tantrums, laughed heartily when he made fun of them; and was herself in return very amusing about Caroline. "Really she seems inclined to behave better," she writes once, "and is only troublesome in private and a great bore in public. This I know you never *could* believe. But I hope some day to see you undergo a dinner when she is trying to show off." Subtlely she tried to discredit Caroline in his eyes; sensibly she pointed out how awkward the connection was likely to prove in the future. Would it not be better—and kinder too—to make an end of it at once?

Lady Melbourne was not alone in her efforts. Lady Bessborough, beside herself with worry, was even more active. But her very amiability made her less effective. Refined and tender-hearted, her only policy in such cases was to appeal to people's better feelings. From Caroline to Byron, from Byron to Byron's friends she hurried, protesting with tears that she knew what a sacrifice she was asking; but that she was sure they would see it was the right thing to do. Further, she could not bear that Caroline should be wounded more than necessary. Let her if possible make the first move: and let them part in no sordid squabble, but with the dignity and considerateness befitting the end of a great love. Such an attitude showed a complete failure to grasp the unbridled irresponsibility of the two people with whom she was dealing. Far rougher measures were needed to make any impression on Caroline; while Byron merely thought Lady Bessborough, or Lady Blarney, as he called her, a foolish sentimentalist. "I am sure Lady B.," he told Lady Melbourne, "will be a little provoked, if I am the first to change, for, like the Governor of Tilbury Fort, although the Countess is resolved, the mother *intenerisce un poco,* and doubtless will expect her daughter to be adored (like an Irish lease) for a term of 99 years."

Behind the two mothers-in-law clamoured a host of secondary advisers. Caroline's conduct had created so resounding a scandal that everyone remotely connected with her—from her brother down to her mother's maid—considered they had a right to interfere. Even Lord Melbourne was roused. As usual a little muddled, he got hold of the idea that Lady Bessborough as well as Caroline was in love with Byron. "They make a fool of me by forcing me to ask him to my house," he lamented to the Prince Regent. Lady Bessborough, informed of the remark, forgot her worries for a moment in a fit of uncontrollable laughter.

Amid all this hullabaloo, one person remained quiet, William. Alone among those closely concerned, he realized the essential unreality of the situation. It was long since he had believed in Caroline's grand passions; and his sharp eye soon perceived that Byron's was no more sincere. The famous Byronic charm had not worked on him. He admitted Byron was handsome and amusing. But he thought his expression unpleasant and his agreeability an uncertain quantity: while himself genuinely well-bred, genuinely detached, genuinely disillusioned, he was not taken in by Byron's pretence of these qualities. As for his Childe Harold airs, William thought them ludicrous affectations: he enjoyed making fun of them to the infuriated Caroline. But he was sure that two such poseurs would never do anything that would seriously endanger their popularity with their public. The idea that they might elope—which haunted Lady Bessborough—did not worry him for a moment. "They neither wish nor intend going," he said, "but both like the fear and interest they create." It was only a repetition of the Webster affair. In indolent, mocking silence, William waited for it to end as quickly.

However, even without his assistance, the family pressure soon grew so strong as to plunge the hero and heroine of the drama into a tumult of perturbation. Byron felt torn in two. By now he cursed the day he ever met Caroline: but he could not face the idea of a clean break. It meant surrendering a conquest, and it would involve a painful scene. Besides, he did not like being unkind if he could help it. All he could bring himself to do was to try and cool her down by urging self-control. Nothing could have been more futile. Caroline was even more divided against herself than he was. Every breath of disapproval stung her like the lash of a whip; on the other hand she was prepared to suffer anything, rather than lose Byron. Under the strain of her mingled feelings, her words took on the wild intensity of tragic poetry. "You think me weak and selfish, you think I did not struggle to withstand my feelings. But it is indeed expecting more than human nature can bear. When I came in last night—when I heard your name announced—the moment after I heard nothing more. . . . How very pale you are, a statue of white marble, and the dark hair and brow, such a contrast. I could never see you without wishing to cry."

At home she acted as though frantic. Lady Melbourne, summoned upstairs by the sound of Caroline's cries, would find her prone on the floor in hysterical sobs. The climax was reached on the morning of 13th August. Lady Bessborough, calling at Melbourne House, found Lord Melbourne deathly pale, screaming to the servants to stop Caroline. She had, it appeared, in a fit of temper, told him she intended to go to Byron. "Go and be damned," he had retorted, "but I don't think he'll take you." Before he had finished speaking, she had rushed, hatless and without a penny, into the street. Poor Lady Bessborough, almost out of her mind, drove all day up and down London searching for Caroline—in vain. It was not till late that night that Caroline was brought home by Byron, who had found her in a surgeon's house at Kensington; preparing, on the proceeds of a ring she had pawned, immediately to set sail she did not know where, on the first ship she could find.

Clearly such an episode must not be repeated. After a hasty consultation between the two families, it was decided that her family should take her and William on a round of visits to Ireland. Alas, it was easier said than done. Caroline, now to all appearance abjectly repentant, professed complete submission. But when it actually came to making a move, at once she began to raise difficulties. She was too ill, her mother was too ill, wouldn't it do as well if she just went to Brocket? And though promising again and again not to communicate with Byron, she met him secretly, and wrote to him three times a day. He, for his part, while assuring Lady Melbourne that he never wished to see Caroline again, lingered on in London; and answered her letters with protestations of constancy, in which he explained that any apparent coldness was only assumed, to quiet the suspicions of her relations. Lady Bessborough, now almost desperate, demanded that William should act. But William provokingly still refused to take the affair seriously. At heart he did not want to. Much suffering at Caroline's hands had forced him to grow a shell of smiling indifference, which he shrank from breaking. Besides, though he saw through her completely, she still had the power to get round him.

After a little cajoling, she had him laughing and reading her mother's letters aloud to her.

There was also a more serious reason for his inertia. Caroline's conduct had not been the only sorrow of his married life. His child, Augustus, within two or three years of his birth, had begun to show unmistakable signs of mental deficiency. Since then Caroline had twice had a miscarriage. To William, so dependent on family affection and so tragically disappointed of it in his wife, all this came as a great blow. Now Caroline—whether seriously or as an excuse to stay in England, it would be uncharitable for posterity to decide—told him that she was once more with child. Rather than risk an accident to the unborn baby, William was prepared to yield to her everything she asked. It seemed as if they would never get away. However, at last Byron announced that he was leaving for Cheltenham. Caroline's motive for staying was removed: her interesting condition mysteriously disappeared: by the end of August the whole party was safely across the Irish Channel.

They were far from the end of their troubles though. Caroline was the most trying holiday companion that can be imagined. The wear and tear of the last few months had intensified her nervous instability as never before; her moods now changed, not every day but every hour. Sometimes she seemed completely her old enchanting self. "Hart and C.," writes Lady Bessborough from Lismore Castle, where they were staying with her cousin Hartington, "had many disputes on the damp, when last night she suddenly opened the door very wide, saying, 'pray walk in, Sir. I have no doubt that you are the rightful possessor, and my cousin only an interloper, usurping your usual habitation.' For a long time nothing came, when at last with great solemnity and many poses, in hopped a *frog,* Caroline following with two candles to treat the master of the castle with proper respect, she said."

Elsewhere she was the breath and soul of the social life of the neighbourhood, flirting outrageously with the local men and footing it in the Irish jig with untiring spirit. But the very same evening the household might be kept up ministering to her, as she screamed and swooned and lay drumming with her heels on the floor. At one moment she would lament her torturing, incurable love for Byron; the next with equal vehemence, she asserted that it was William alone who had always possessed her heart; and she delighted to caress him in front of other people. The whole countryside talked of how fond Lady Caroline seemed of her husband. "When they say this to me," remarked the exasperated Lady Bessborough, "I want to bellow."

The unfortunate William might well have bellowed

too. For on him fell the brunt of Caroline's hysteria. If she could not sleep, she woke him up; when he suggested going alone to Dublin for a few days, she fell into transports of agitation, swearing that, if he did, she would never see him again. However, he rose to the occasion. In the sustained intimacy of country life he began to realize how serious her condition was. And, with this realization, the unselfish tenderness of his nature came to the surface. He devoted himself to her with a patience and sympathy that brought tears to Lady Bessborough's eyes; gave up going to Dublin without a word of protest; sat up till daybreak three nights running, holding her head in order to soothe her. On one occasion only is he recorded to have betrayed the strain he was feeling. During one of Caroline's nocturnal paroxysms, a deafening thunder-storm burst out. "The storm outside," said William to her with a rueful humour, "is hardly more than that inside."

Meanwhile Byron, on the other side of the sea, was showing himself equally unstable. He had bidden farewell to Caroline with words of undying fidelity. "All will be done to make you change," he said, "but it is only you I am afraid for; for myself there is no fear." And for the first few weeks after she had left he wrote to her lovingly. But by the same post he also sent letters to Lady Melbourne saying that all was finally over between them, and talking airily of other flirtations. Lady Melbourne, always anxious to make trouble between them, duly reported his words to Caroline. Immediately torrents of accusation, lamenting, and abuse began to pour over from Ireland on his head. From force of habit he denied Lady Melbourne's reports. But as a matter of fact he was glad enough of an occasion for quarrel. Caroline's absence had made him realize how delightfully quiet life could be without her. By the end of August he had made up his mind he must be free of her before she came back.

His best method seemed to be to involve himself with another woman. Accordingly, prompted partly by Lady Melbourne, he sent a proposal of marriage to her niece, Miss Annabella Milbanke. Miss Milbanke refused him: with a certain relief, Byron turned to less responsible forms of love. And by the middle of October, he was up to the neck in an affair with Caroline's old friend, Lady Oxford. It seems odd that he should have left one professional romantic for another. But Lady Oxford's romanticism was very different from Caroline's, a fashionable pose that had no connection with the cool and easy-going sensuality which in fact directed her conduct. "A broken heart is nothing but a bad digestion," she told Byron; and in her company he could relax to enjoy the pleasures of the body, safe from fear of subsequent scenes and heart-burnings. Only Lady Oxford exacted one condition in return for her favours. Relations with Caroline must be broken off finally, and at once.

Byron did not hesitate. Apart from his own irritation with Caroline, the same weakness that had kept him so long tied to her, now made him wax in Lady Oxford's hands. But, like all weak people when driven at last to take a strong line, he lost his head and acted far too violently. In a tremble of fear lest he should lose his new-found tranquillity, and determined by one blow to save himself from any further trouble with Caroline, he wrote off to her, without any preliminary warning, the most unforgivable letter he could concoct. "As to yourself, Lady Caroline," it ended, "correct your vanity which has become ridiculous—exert your caprices on others, enjoy the excellent flow of spirits which make you so delightful in the eyes of others, and leave me in peace." Caroline, receiving this incredible document at the Dolphin Hotel, Dublin, whence she was preparing to set sail for England, took to her bed for a fortnight in a state of nervous convulsions.

It was the end, as far as any hope for her was concerned. Byron, once free, was never going to allow himself to fall into her clutches again. But it was not in Caroline to face an unpleasant fact. And for the next six months she fought a desperate rearguard action, if not to win him back, at any rate to remain a leading figure in his life. Indeed, even less than usual was she in a condition to listen to reason. Byron's letter had thrown her already tottering mind, for the time being, completely off its balance. Ghastly pale, bone-thin, and with eyes starting from her head, she looked insane; and throughout the winter, derangement also betrayed itself in a series of actions, fantastic, ludicrous and distressing. She offered herself to young men on condition that they challenge Byron to a duel; she forged a letter from Byron to a picture-dealer in order to get possession of his portrait; she put her men servants into a new livery, on the buttons of which were engraved "Ne crede Byron"—Do not believe Byron. But her most singular performance was a bonfire at Brocket, on which Byron's presents to her were solemnly burnt; whilst some village girls dressed in white capered round the flames in a ritual dance of triumph, and a page recited verses composed by Caroline for the occasion.

"Ah look not thus on me," so they adjured her audience, "So grave and sad.

"Shake not your heads nor say the lady's mad."
They did say so, nevertheless.

Meanwhile she continued to bombard Byron with menaces of vengeance—"Very like the style of Lucy in the Beggar's Opera," said Byron, "and by no means hav-

ing the merit of novelty in my ears"—incoherently interspersed with agonized pleadings for some sign of re-
lenting; a letter, a bracelet of his hair, above all an interview.

Some time in the spring the interview did take place.
According to Caroline it was very affecting; Byron, bathed
in tears, implored her forgiveness. But it is difficult to
believe this in the light of the letters he wrote about her
to others. For the time being at any rate he positively
hated her. Exasperation at her persecution of him had
called up all that ultimate antagonism to women which
childish misfortune had implanted at the root of his
character. On Caroline he visited all the sins of her
worthless and predatory sex. He replied to her appeals
with studied cruelty, and answered her request for a bracelet, first by sending one made of Lady Oxford's hair,
which happened to be the same colour as his own; and
then by relating the deception as an excellent joke to all
his friends, including Lady Melbourne. What made him
particularly angry was that the noise created by the affair
was doing him harm socially. Caroline abused him as
loudly as he abused her: some people believed her; as
the year advanced, Byron, always sensitive to public
opinion, began to notice a party was forming against
him. "With regard to the miseries of 'this correct and
animated waltzer,' as *The Morning Post* entitles her," he

complained to Lady Melbourne, "I wish she would not call in the aid of so many compassionate countesses. There is Lady W. (with a tongue, too) conceives me to be the greatest barbarian since the days of Bacchus; and all who hate Lady Oxford—consisting of one half of the world, and all who abominate me—that is the other half—will tear the last rag of my tattered reputation into threds, filaments and atoms."

Scandal had yet to reach its climax. On 5th July, Byron and Caroline met at a ball given by Lady Heathcote. It was the first time they had been together in society, since the previous summer: and Caroline arrived, determined to make one last effort to rekindle Byron's flame. She went straight up to him; and in order to pique his jealousy, said, "I presume *now* I am allowed to waltz." He replied, with contempt, that she could do as she liked, as far as he was concerned. And a few dances later, brushing past her in a doorway, "I have been admiring your dexterity," he whispered sarcastically. Wild with rage, and resolved in revenge to bring him to public shame at whatever cost to herself, she rushed into the supper-room; and, breaking a glass, began to gash her naked arms with the pieces. Immediately the place was in a tumult; women screamed; only Lady Melbourne, with her usual presence of mind, seized Caroline's hands and held her down. A few minutes later, still jabbing at herself with a pair of scissors, she was carried from the room.* Lady Melbourne reserved her comments for Byron's ears. "She is now like a Barrel of Gunpowder and takes fire with the most trifling spark. She has been in a dreadfull—I was interrupted & obliged to put my paper into my drawer, & now I cannot for my life recollect what I was going to say—oh now I have it!—I was stating tht. she had been in a dreadful bad humour this last week. With her, when the fermentation begins there is no stopping it till it bursts forth. . . . I must do Ly. Bessborough the justice to say that her representation of her violence in these paroxysms was not at all exaggerated. I could not have believed it possible for any one to carry absurdity to such a pitch. I call it so, for I am convinced she knows perfectly what she is about all the time, but she has no idea of controlling her fury." Byron was quick to reply to this communication in a similarly scornful strain. But secretly he could not help feeling gratified at having been the occasion of so memorable a scene. After his death, carefully preserved among his papers, was found a faded invitation card to the party. "This card I keep as a curiosity," he had scribbled on it,

* There are several accounts of this celebrated episode—by Byron, by Caroline, by Lady Melbourne and by various social gossips of the period— agreeing in the main but differing in detail. When in doubt I follow Lady Melbourne. She had more chance of knowing the truth than the gossips and less motive than Byron or Caroline for misrepresenting it.

"for it was at this ball that Lady C. L. performed ye dagger scene—of indifferent memory."

Next day London was ringing with the incident. A scandal was just what was needed to revive the excitement of a dying season; and such a scandal! Everywhere the story was told and re-told, each time with some new dramatic detail added; letters of condolence poured in on the outraged Lamb family; a scurrilous paper, *The Satirist,* published a leading article on the subject. The uproar grew so violent that it became impossible for Caroline to remain in London. She was packed off to spend the rest of the summer at Brocket.

It was a turning point in her life. Up till now, though she had shocked public opinion, she had always managed not to put herself outside the pale of society. The cousin of the Duke of Devonshire, the wife of William Lamb, was allowed to get away with a great deal that would have ruined a less glorious personage. Caroline's paroxysms of actual violence, too, had always been kept relatively private. But now she had given way to one in public; she had also published her infidelity to her husband in a way that not even Lady Oxford had ever done. And though the influence of her friends still kept her from being made an open outcast, for the rest of her life she was a marked woman.

She felt it with all the force of her nature. "I see the

sharp censures ready to start into words in every cold, formal face I meet," she cried. And people noted that for the first time she showed genuine signs of shame. It was not only that she was tormented by the consciousness of other people's disapproval; a death blow had been struck at the security of that palace of illusions in which alone she could happily live. At last she had managed to involve herself in a scene as spectacular as any in poetry or romance. And what had been the effect on the world? Not admiration, not even sympathy; but harsh disapprobation and derisive contempt. Such a catastrophe made its impression. No longer could she persuade herself that the world thought her the heroine she wished to be. A subtle change began to penetrate her outlook. That supreme self-confidence, which had enabled her to survive so many setbacks, for the first time began to give way.

It was left to William to administer such comfort as could be found. Poor William! One wonders what his thoughts were. But history tantalizingly is silent; and perhaps he never gave them utterance. Throughout the long ordeal of the preceding winter he had maintained to the outward world his shell of apparent indifference. "William Lamb laughs, and eats like a trooper," said an observer who saw him on their return from Ireland. And during the events that followed, during all Caroline's bonfires and forgeries, he continued, as far as we can gather, to eat and laugh. Caroline professed herself very much hurt, that he, in particular, should not have fought a duel on her behalf; she said that it would have brought her back to him. And it is possible that some such picturesque gesture might for a moment have revived her romantic interest. But it was not in William to make gestures. And besides, he did not think they would do any good. By now he had few illusions left about her; certainly he thought it was no use trying to control her vagaries. All the same, he would not cut himself completely free from her. His family wanted him to. Furious at the disgrace which "the little beast" had brought upon them, from this time on they were always pressing him to get a separation. But he refused. It came partly from the same apathy that stopped him trying to influence her actions: it came also from pity. Ever since Ireland, he had felt so sorry for her that he could not help being lenient. After all, he tried to persuade himself, she should not be blamed too much; the trouble was chiefly Byron's fault.

William's pent-up feelings showed themselves in a bitter, steadily growing hatred of Byron. That he should have seduced Caroline was bad enough; but that he should turn against her afterwards was even more shocking to his honourable spirit. When he heard that Byron was threatening to cut her publicly, all William's own injuries at her hands were forgotten in a sudden flare of indignation. Byron thought this very inconsistent of him. But it was Byron's misfortune not to appreciate the workings of a generous nature. Nor would he have understood why William resented his relationship to Lady Melbourne. To William it was acutely painful that his own mother should have so little sense of his feelings as to conspire against his wife with that wife's lover. Only here again affection made him put the chief responsibility on Byron. With the sharp eye of hatred, he penetrated, as Lady Melbourne had failed to do, the essential duplicity of Byron's character. "He was treacherous beyond conception," he said in later years. "I believe he was fond of treachery. He dazzled everybody and deceived them: for he could tell his own story very well." To desert the victim of such a ruffian, at the moment when she was desolate, was against William's most sacred instincts. If he could not leave the Whig party when its fortunes were at a low ebb, how much less could he leave his own wife. For the next two years he hardly quitted her side.

People noticed that grey streaks were appearing in his black curls. No wonder; it must have been a dreadful strain. Caroline, though at first a little subdued by misfortune, was no more rational than before; her moods still varied between wild gaiety, fits of rage and bursts of tears. Miss Webb, a companion who had been engaged to help look after her, recommended that she should play the harp, which she considered a sovereign remedy for mental disorders. Whether she was right must remain doubtful. For Caroline would not look at the harp. She preferred the organ, on which she would play all night, till she was frozen with cold. She also kept the house awake, by stalking the passages like a ghost, till the early hours of the morning. In the daytime she often refused to eat. William bore it all as best he could. Sometimes his temper broke out. "It is too bad of you," he would cry out. "If you fret so, I will send you to live with your grandmother." The graceful rooms which had provided so harmonious a setting for the careless sunshine of their honeymoon hours, now resounded all too often with Caroline's wails, with William's oaths and exasperated laughter. And from his relations at any rate he no longer tried to hide what he thought of Caroline's character. "When Mr. C. spoke to Caroline about the road," we find him writing to his mother, "she was too happy in the opportunity of at once abusing them, and making an excuse for herself."

But on the whole he was extraordinarily patient and sympathetic. He made the most of her rare moments of good humour; if her depression became intense, he

THE YOUNG MELBOURNE

could be absolutely depended upon to give support and comfort. And for the rest he took advantage of his leisure to meditate and study.

Now and again, they made a brief excursion into the great world. We catch a sight of them during the summer of 1814 at a masquerade ball given in honour of the victory over Napoleon, at Wattier's Club; William handsome, but a little self-conscious, in a costume of conspicuous splendour; Caroline prancing about in green pantaloons—"masked," said Byron, a sardonic observer of the couple, "but always trying to indicate who she was to everybody." The following May they were abroad for several months. Caroline's brother, Frederick, had been wounded at Waterloo; so she hurried out to Brussels, her fancy fired by the picture of herself as ministering angel at the bedside of a hero. In practice, however, she found it boring; and preferred to promenade the streets of Brussels; where she shocked Miss Burney, by appearing with arms, shoulders and back bare, but for a floating scarf of gauze.

We next hear of the Lambs in Paris, during its triumphant occupation by the allies. "Nobody is agissant but Caroline William in a purple riding habit, tormenting everybody," writes her cousin Harriet, now wife of the English Ambassador, Lord Granville, "but, I am convinced, ready primed for an attack on the Duke of Wel-

180

lington; and I have no doubt but that she will to a certain extent succeed, as no dose of flattery is too strong for him to swallow or her to administer. Poor William hides in a small room, while she assembles lovers and tradespeople in another. He looks worn to the bone."

Lady Granville was right in her prophecies. Caroline was still sufficiently her old self to be stirred to instant pursuit of the acknowledged hero of Europe: the Duke was at once gratified by her adulation and amused by her oddness. The next glimpse we get of her, she is giving occasional "screams of delight" as she dines alone with him and Sir Walter Scott.

Indeed the whole world seemed to be in Paris. Every night the Lambs were out meeting distinguished personages, Talleyrand, Metternich, Lord Castlereagh, Kings and Queens. William enjoyed it all. It appealed to his interest both in historic events and public characters. He sought to improve his appearance by having his grey hairs pulled out: and never went to bed before four in the morning. Caroline, too, was in a good humour with him. "Whom do you imagine I consider the most distinguished man I ever met?" she suddenly asked a neighbour at dinner. "Lord Byron," he replied tentatively. "No, my own husband, William Lamb," said Caroline.

Her good humour, however, was not to be depended upon. A Mr. and Mrs. Kemble met the Lambs at dinner one night with Lord Holland, "when accidentally the expected arrival of Lord Byron was mentioned," writes their daughter. "Mr. Lamb had just named the next day as the one fixed for their departure, but Lady Caroline immediately announced her intention of prolonging her stay, which created what would be called in French chambers 'sensation.' When the party broke up, my father and mother, who occupied apartments in the same hotel as the Lambs—Meurice's—were driven into the courtyard, just as Lady Caroline's carriage had drawn up before the staircase leading to her rooms. . . . A *ruisseau,* or gutter, ran round the courtyard, and intervened between the carriage step and the door of the vestibule, and Mr. Lamb, taking Lady Caroline, as she alighted in his arms (she had a very pretty, slight, graceful figure) gallantly lifted her over the wet stones. . . . My mother's sitting-room faced that of Lady Caroline and before lights were brought into it she and my father had the full benefit of a curious scene in the room of their opposite neighbours. Mr. Lamb, on entering the room, sat down on the sofa, and his wife perched herself on the end of it, with her arm round his neck, which engaging attitude she presently exchanged for a still more persuasive air, by kneeling at his feet, but upon his getting up, the lively lady did so also, and in a moment began flying round the room,

seizing and flinging on the floor, cups, saucers, plates—
the whole cabaret, vases, candlesticks, etc., her poor husband pursuing and attempting to restrain his mad moiety,
in the midst of which extraordinary scene the curtains
were abruptly closed, and the domestic drama finished
behind them, leaving no doubt, however, in my father
and mother's minds, that the question of Lady Caroline's
prolonged stay till Lord Byron's arrival in Paris had
caused the disturbance they had witnessed."

Indeed, for all she might say, she had never brought
herself to give up hope of getting Byron back. At times
the scales did fall from her eyes. Byron, she told a friend,
would have stuck to her, if she had been celebrated
enough as a beauty to be a credit to him. But such moments of insight into his true nature were fleeting; she
could not for long give up her intoxicating dream. He
was still deluged at intervals with spates of letters from
her: during her visit to London in the summer of 1814,
she once more took to haunting his rooms. On one occasion she created a great deal of embarrassment by suddenly bursting in dressed up as a carman, at a moment
when he was intimately entertaining another lady. On
another he came home to find the words "Remember
me" scrawled in Caroline's hand on a book that lay on
the writing-table.

"Remember thee," he wrote, "remember thee!
   Till Lethe quench life's burning streams
Remorse and shame shall cling to thee
   And haunt thee like a feverish dream.

Remember thee! Ay, doubt it not,
   Thy husband too shall think of thee,
By neither shalt thou be forgot,
   Thou false to him, thou fiend to me!"

To Lady Melbourne he lamented in a less stormy strain, but with equal irritation. "You talk to me about keeping her out. It is impossible, she comes in at all times, at any time; the moment the door is open, in she walks. I cannot throw her out of the window."

He felt very much inclined to. When she was badgering him, he hated her as much as ever. But he was inconstant in hate as in love. If Caroline was quiet for a month or two, dislike of losing his power over her would combine with a genuine impulse of affection, to produce a fitful revulsion in his feelings. He wrote to her kindly; he even felt a curious desire to see her again.

In such circumstances they continued to meet on and off, for at least eight months more. In the spring of 1814 they had a scene of farewell at his rooms; when, so Caroline says, Byron confided to her such dreadful revelations about himself, that she vowed never to see him again. But, in view of her previous history, it is extremely unlikely she would have kept this vow, had not Byron a few months later got engaged to Miss Milbanke. Certainly he was in a fever lest the announcement of the engagement should provoke one of Caroline's old explosions. However, for a wonder she kept fairly quiet, contenting herself with telling other people that "Byron would never pull together with a woman who went to church punctually, understood statistics, and had a bad figure."

She was quite right, it needed less than a year to prove it. The crash, when it came, gave Caroline a last chance to display to her lover the bewildering contradictions of her nature. There is reason for thinking that it was she who spread abroad those reports of Byron's intrigue with his sister, which made any reconciliation with his wife finally impossible. On the other hand, to Byron himself Caroline wrote urging moderation and magnanimity; and even offered to tell Lady Byron that any stories she was told against Byron had been invented by herself— Caroline—out of jealousy. Was this offer just a final theatrical gesture: or did she, confronted for once by a real tragedy, rise above her egotism to that level of heroic self-sacrifice to which she professed to aspire? Either is possible. As it was the last communication she ever held with Byron, we may be allowed to give her the benefit of the doubt.

Chapter VII

FRUSTRATION

LAS, THERE was no doubt about her behaviour to the rest of the world. In spite of William and Miss Webb, Caroline's condition of mind during the last two years had progressively deteriorated. The disaster at Lady Heathcote's ball had finally undermined her belief in her illusions; she had realized her failure there, too keenly for her to be able ever again to play the role of heroine with her old confidence in its success. Yet her vanity was too fundamental for her to be able to profit by the stern lessons of experience. She could not face the fact that she was wrong; so she was unable to reform herself. Instead, bewildered, terrified and resentful, she rushed blindly about, seeking, she hardly knew how, to put her shattered day-dreams together again. At times, as we have seen, she made futile efforts to behave with her former self-assurance; chased after the Duke of Wellington, paraded the streets of Brussels half naked. But for the most part, she stayed at home where, surrounded by a swarm of page boys whom she alternately spoiled and bullied, she tried to forget her gnawing sense of shame by indulging every whim of fancy, yielding to every gust of distraught temper. Her eccentricities grew more and more marked, her tantrums wilder than ever before. It became growingly impossible to live with her. The breaking-point was reached in April, 1816, when, provoked by some trifling act of mischief on the part of one of her pages, she flung a ball so hard at his head that it drew blood. "Oh, my Lady, you've killed me!" he cried out. "Oh, God!" she yelled, tearing out into the hall, "I have murdered the page."

As a matter of fact he was hardly hurt. But there was no telling, the Lambs felt, what might happen next time. Caroline was certainly a lunatic, and probably a dangerous one. They made up their minds that it was impossible for William to live with her any longer. In a body they went to William and once more demanded a separation. This time he did not refuse.

Formal separations, however, entail lengthy preliminaries. For three weeks Melbourne House was made hideous by a succession of appalling scenes, in which the Lambs told Caroline, with brutal frankness, that she was mad, and she in return now stormed, now pleaded. Neither was of any avail: the arrangements went inexorably on. Beside herself with fury and despair, Caroline resolved on revenge. Before she was cast out of the house, she would at least publish her story to the world in such a way, as to justify herself and confound her enemies. Accordingly, dressed for some mysterious reason in page's costume, she proceeded to sit up day and night writing. Some weeks later an old copyist called Woodhouse was summoned to Melbourne House, where, to his astonishment, he was confronted by what he took at first to be a boy of fourteen, who presented him with the manuscript of a novel. Before the end of May this novel, *Glenarvon,* made its appearance on the book-sellers' tables.

It is a deplorable production: an incoherent cross between a realistic novel of fashionable life and a fantastic tale of terror, made preposterous by every absurd device—assassins, spectres, manacled maniacs, children changed at birth—that an imagination nurtured on mock-Gothic romance could suggest. But it has its interest, as revealing the way that Caroline contrived to reshape her story so as to please her vanity. She appears as Calantha, a heroine, noble, innocent, fascinating, but too impulsive for success in a hard-hearted world. Her husband, Lord Avondale, otherwise William, in spite of the fact that he too is unusually noble-hearted, neglects her, and corrupts her morals by his cynical views. In consequence, she yields to the temptations of a depraved society and finally, though only after heroic resistance on her part, is seduced by Byron, here called Glenarvon. He is Byronism incarnate; beautiful and gifted beyond belief, but driven by the pangs of a conscience burdened with inexpiable crimes, to go about betraying and ruining people in a spirit of gloomy desperation. Though Calantha is the love of his life, he deserts her out of pure devilry. The heartless world turns against her; she dies of a broken heart: Avondale dies shortly afterwards out of sympathy. For Glenarvon a more sensational fate is reserved. He jumps off a ship into the sea after sailing about for days, pursued by a phantom vessel manned by revengeful demons of gigantic size.

The tension of this dramatic tale is relieved by some thinly veiled satirical portraits of the Lamb family, the Devonshire family, Lady Oxford, Lady Holland, and a number of other leading social figures, notably the influential Lady Jersey. Its moral is that Caroline's misfortunes were Byron's fault, William's fault, society's fault—anyone's fault, in fact, but her own.

The world did not accept this view. *Glenarvon* had a

success of scandal; three editions were called for within a few weeks. But it dealt the death blow to what remained of Caroline's social position. Ever since Lady Heathcote's ball she had kept it on sufferance; certain people had continued to countenance her out of affection for her relations. Now she had set out deliberately, and in print, to insult these last of her supporters. It is not surprising that they too turned against her. In desperate bravado she had continued to go into society, at the time the book was appearing; only to find that her cousins avoided her, Lord Holland cut her dead, and Lady Jersey scratched her name off the list of Almack's Club. At last she had succeeded in putting herself completely outside the pale. And she was never to get inside it again.

As for the Lambs, they were almost out of their minds. For many years, so they not unjustifiably considered, they had endured Caroline's goings-on with singular patience. And in return she had chosen to wound them in their two tenderest points, family loyalty and regard for appearances. To people brought up with Lady Melbourne's tradition of discretion, no worse torment can be imagined, than to have the intimacies of family life displayed in public. And in such an unfavourable light! What cause for odious triumph would the book not give to that dowdy and envious section of society which had always maligned them? While, when they thought what their beloved William must be feeling as he saw *Glenarvon* lying open on the tables of every house he entered, their fury almost suffocated them.

Caroline was impenitent. William, she asserted, had enjoyed the book very much. That she should have succeeded in persuading herself of this, is the most extraordinary of all her extraordinary feats of self-deception. In fact William was utterly crushed. He had heard nothing of the book till the morning of its appearance. "Caroline," he said, coming into her room, "I have stood your friend till now—I even think you were ill-used: but if it is true that this novel is published—and as they say against us all—I will never see you more."

That all the long-concealed shames and sorrows of his marriage should be dragged out for the world to see, was torture to a man of his sensitive reserve; it was also acutely distressing that one, closely connected with him, should behave with such treacherous ingratitude to those he loved. Sunk in black gloom he sat all day in Melbourne House; "I wish I was dead," he muttered. "I wish I was dead." And to his old friends the Hollands he wrote off such halting words of apology as he could find:

"Dear Holland,

It must have appeared strange to you that I have not been to see you. And you may perhaps put a

wrong construction on it—it is nothing but the embarrassment which the late events have not unnaturally
revived. They have given me great trouble and vexa-
tion, and produced an unwillingness to see anybody
and more particularly those who have been the objects
of so wanton and unprofitable an attack. I did not
write, because, what could I say? I could only excul-
pate myself from any previous knowledge, the effect of
which must be to throw a heavier burden on the offending party—I am sure you will feel for my situation. I
should like to see you some morning. Yours W.L."

The grounds for separation seemed stronger than ever.
Indeed, several people wrote to William saying that if he
did not now break with Caroline, they would consider it
a sign that he connived at her book. By the middle of
the summer the arrangements were pretty well completed.
The evening before the final signature, William, leaving
Caroline, as he thought, in safe hands, went down to
Brocket for a night's quiet. What was his dismay, while
he was undressing, to hear a scuffling noise outside his
room. It was Caroline, who had escaped, followed him
down, and was preparing to make a last desperate effort
to melt his stony heart by spending the night stretched
out on his door-mat. What transpired between them is
unknown. But next morning the lawyers, arriving with

the papers, found her sitting on his knee in fits of laughter, feeding him with small scraps of bread and butter.
The Deed of Separation was a dead letter.

What was the reason for this surprising change of
heart? Caroline no doubt thought it was simply love.
And it is true that all his sufferings at her hands had not
succeeded in driving her image wholly from William's
heart. The same incurable immaturity of spirit which
made her behave so childishly, also kept her charm fresh.
When for a moment the storm clouds of hysteria parted,
it sparkled out as waywardly captivating as ever: and
against his will, William responded to it. But it would
seem that his volte-face was due primarily to other and
more complex motives. Dislike of the unpleasant had
something to do with it; he could not bring himself to
face the agonizing ordeal of a final scene of farewell.
He felt guilty too; at the back of his mind lurked an uneasy feeling that his carelessness during the early days
of their marriage was partly responsible for her present
collapse. But strangely enough, he was most of all affected by *Glenarvon*. He might say, in the first heat of
anger, that he never meant to see her again: but when the
full storm broke, when he saw everyone cutting her, when
he read the outrageous personal attacks on her published
in the newspapers, his mood underwent a revulsion. Bad
as Caroline might be, she was not so bad as to deserve

such persecution. Besides, if he had felt it shabby to leave her before, how much more now! Except for him, she had not a friend in the world. Every chivalrous instinct, every touching memory of his old love, revolted against deserting her in such a plight. Once more personal obligation showed itself the one strong motive for action in his frustrated nature. "Caroline," he told her, "we will stand or fall together."

Most likely they would fall. It is not to be imagined that William entered on this new chapter of his wedded life with rosy expectations. However, he had long ago given up expecting much of anything. Drama, as usually happens in real life, had ended not in tragic denouement, but in lassitude and anti-climax. In pity, in exasperation, in ironical apathy, he settled down to his accustomed round.

Elsewhere also he was beginning to pick up old threads again. In the spring he had re-entered the House of Commons. Ever since he had left, his friends had been urging him to come back; and in 1815 Lord Holland had written offering him a seat. But for the time being William had lost his zest for Parliamentary life. The more philosophical outlook afforded by the windows of Brocket library made the bustle of party politics look a futile waste of energy. Anyhow, he did not want to come back as a Holland House man. Since peace had been signed, the

Foxites had shown themselves more academically out of touch with reality than ever. Though Europe was still shaking, they wanted most of the army dismissed at once, for fear it might lead to a Cromwellian military despotism; they worried lest by helping to restore the French king, the English Government had implied belief in the divine right of kings. Worst of all in William's eyes, at a time when every sensible person was longing only for peace and quiet, they were toying with subversive schemes of reform. The detachment in which William had been living made him more confident in his independent views. In a letter of refusal to Lord Holland, he made his position thoroughly clear. "In the present state of politics with no one in either House of Parliament whom I should choose to follow, with questions, certain to occur, so numerous and so various, so perplexed by circumstances and complicated in the detail, that it is almost impossible for any two persons to come to the same conclusion upon all of them, it would be very disagreeable and embarrassing for me to have a seat in the House of Commons which should not allow me the fullest and most unquestioned liberty of acting upon any subject according to my own particular opinion—I cannot also conceal from myself that the having been 3 years without taking any part in public affairs has had the natural effect to a certain degree of diminishing the eagerness of the interest which

I once felt in them; and consideration and reflection have had the equally natural effect of altering and, in my view, amending some of the opinions which I fancied myself to hold. . . In Europe I am for an immediate settlement even though that settlement be full of errors and imperfections; because I cannot but think I perceive that every fresh struggle and convulsion in France or Spain or elsewhere, only terminates in impairing and diminishing justice, liberty and all real rights, or rather the real interests of mankind. Such being my opinions . . . I apprehend they will force you to come to the same conclusion as myself, that such a political connection would only lead to mutual dissatisfaction and reproach . . . my principles are I believe the Whig principles of the Revolution; the main foundation of these is the irresponsibility of the crown, the consequent responsibility of Ministers, the preservation of the power and dignity of Parliament as constituted by Law and Custom. With a heap of modern additions and interpolations I have nothing to do—with those who maintain those principles and against those who either do or appear to be ready to sacrifice them, I shall always act; but I must always lament when I see the advocates of freedom injure their own cause by raising objections which are inapplicable or extravagant or impracticable as I do beg you to consider. . . .

'ντα λιαν δημοτικα απολυει την δημοκρατιαι.'

FRUSTRATION

However, when a year later he was offered a seat at Northampton that did not commit him to strict party orthodoxy, he accepted it. He had nothing else to do; his family wanted him to; and a vague rumour was afloat that Canning might at last be coming into office.

A doubtful flicker of light illuminated the political horizon. All the same, looked at as a whole, his situation was a cheerless one. And he felt it. This period, and still more the four years preceding it, were the most melancholy of his active life. Brooding aimlessly in the book-lined seclusion of Brocket library, pacing the turfy solitudes of its park in the fading summer twilight, he would be overwhelmed by a leaden sensation of failure, of emptiness, of the fleeting vanity of things human, his own existence most of all. It is not surprising. He was now thirty-seven; and the perspective of his past life that met his eyes as he turned to survey it from the gathering shadows of middle age was, for all its surface glitter, a profoundly disheartening spectacle. The world and his own weaknesses, victorious over him in early years, had now in his maturity more decisively defeated him. He had yielded to the inhibiting pressure of convention and tradition; his creative individuality had forced for itself no outlet; the conflict that lay at the root of his nature had ended by effectively frustrating his power of action. He had indeed gone into Parliament and married. But his marriage, so far from providing him with an independent base from which his personality might develop unhampered, had merely served to sap his spirit and confirm his cynicism. Love had turned out the most painful of all his disillusionments. Further, the misfortunes of his wedded life had intensified that morbid self-protectiveness, that propensity at all costs to avoid trouble, which was a major defect of his character. Nor was his political career a more encouraging subject of contemplation. The most valuable part of him had found no means of expression in the atmosphere of Parliament: while, though he sympathized too little with his party to combat usefully in its cause, he shrank too much from wounding his friends to leave them, and throw in his lot openly with that leader in whom at heart he believed. Alike in public and in private life, he recognized himself as a failure: and there seemed no reason to suppose he would ever be anything else.

It is true that in neither had he ostensibly given up the struggle. He had gone back into the House of Commons: he had reconciled himself with Caroline. But these acts are evidence of his defeat rather than of his fighting spirit. For he was not proposing to attack his old problems with new vigour and by new methods. It was just that he lacked sufficient faith in himself, or in anything else, to try and rebuild his life on fresh lines. Better, in a world of deception and disappointment, to acquiesce in the line of least resistance. If Caroline wanted him, he would stay with her; if Lady Melbourne liked him to be a member of Parliament, a member of Parliament he would be. A distinguished creative intelligence, he resigned himself, unless fortune changed, to live the unfertile life of a commonplace man of his rank. An onlooker in youth, in middle age he settled down to be an onlooker, if need be, for the rest of his days.

Only not with the old zest. He had not lost his curiosity about the world: he could entertain himself with the passing moment pleasantly enough. But with the dissolution of his youthful dreams and aspirations, had vanished also the keen savour of his youthful joys. The rapture of first love, the burning, exultant thirst for truth, the stir of the heart quickened by the tumult and trumpet call of great events—where were they now? Nor had life supplied him with any compensating source of happiness to take their place. William still scribbled verses to wile away a vacant hour: and in a paraphrase from the Latin, made apparently about this time, we may catch a hint of the emotions that welled up in his tired spirit as, pausing at this sad milestone of his life's pilgrimage, he mused on times gone by:

THE YOUNG MELBOURNE

'Tis late, and I must haste away,
My usual hour of rest is near;
And do you press me, youths, to stay—
To stay and revel longer here?

Then give me back the scorn of care
Which spirits light in health allow;
And give me back the dark brown hair
Which curled upon my even brow.

And give me back the sportive jest
Which once could midnight hours beguile,
The life that bounded in my breast,
And joyous youth's becoming smile!

And give me back the fervid soul
Which love inflamed with strange delight,
When erst I sorrowed o'er the bowl
At Chloe's coy and wanton flight.

'Tis late, and I must haste away,
My usual hour of rest is near;
But give me these and I will stay—
Will stay till morn—and revel here!

With regret, with resignation, with hopeless bitter-sweet yearning, he gazed back at his memories of the irretrievable past. There seemed nothing much worth looking at in the future.

PART III

Chapter VIII

TEN YEARS LATER

O N 20TH JUNE, 1826, Emily Lamb, now Countess Cowper, sat writing the family news to her brother Frederick at Madrid where he was Minister Plenipotentiary. "William," ran her letter, "looks cheerful and gay, but is much too fat."

This brief sentence sums up the main changes that were to be observed in him during the years that had elapsed since 1816. William was in better spirits and his figure had begun to fill out; but that was all. The melancholy prognostications of ten years back had been fulfilled; fate had not seen fit to rescue him from the frustrated and stagnant situation in which he had then found himself; at forty-seven his prospects and his position were substantially the same as at thirty-seven.

Politically he was still poised uneasily between Whig and Tory. Those rumours of Canning's imminent triumph, which had raised his hopes on his re-entry into Parliament, had proved illusory. And William settled down to pursue his usual and lonely middle course. During the anxious years that followed the conclusion of peace, he had sometimes supported Government, sometimes Opposition. The riotings and rick-burnings which had disturbed the countryside roused his fear of revolution; and he agreed in 1816 to become a member of the committee appointed to devise means of repressing disorder. Later he voted both for the suspension of Habeas Corpus and for the Six Acts. On the other hand, unlike the Tories, he had been in favour of an enquiry into the Peterloo massacre and had voted for Mackintosh's bill for modifying the rigours of the penal code. Moreover in economic matters he had taken the Whig side; arguing vigorously on behalf of economy and no income tax. As regards foreign affairs he was for keeping quiet. Above all, England should not be so silly as to set up as the moral arbiter of Europe, either on the side of authority or freedom. In 1820 public life was diversified by the unedifying farce of Queen Caroline's divorce. William, along with his fellow Whigs, was against the King, and voted for retaining the Queen's name in the liturgy. But he was too worldly-wise to persuade himself into any romantic belief in her innocence. It would be better for her, he said, to act magnanimously; and he took the trouble to write to the virtuous Mr. Wilberforce asking him to come up in order to try and persuade the King to any compromise which might compose the situation, and so avoid the risk of popular tumults. The juxtaposition of two such incongruous characters as William and Wilberforce provides an entertaining spectacle. Wilberforce liked William, but had a horror of getting mixed up in so disreputable an affair; "oh, the corrupted currents of this world," he confided to his diary, "oh, for that better world where there is no shuffling!" William for his part, though diplomatically polite to so formidable a pillar of respectability, did not find him sympathetic. "I believe he has good motives," he said, "but they are very uncomfortable for those he has to act with." Wilberforce's inner life as revealed a few years later in his published diary William thought ridiculous; "perpetually vexing himself, because he amused himself too well."

In 1821 Canning at last got office; but, by bad luck, it was in such circumstances as to make it no advantage to William. What he wanted was a Whig-Tory Coalition. Canning was now the Tory member of an exclusively Tory administration. Nothing had occurred since William had re-entered Parliament to loosen those bonds of personal loyalty which held him to his old party. And when in 1824 Canning offered him a place, once again he felt bound to refuse. However, though he could not himself join Canning he was all for anyone else doing so. Three years earlier he had strongly urged his friend Ward to accept a similar office. "It would have the effect of supporting and assisting Canning," he remarked, "at this moment, and it might enable you to be of essential service to the Ministry. At the same time," he adds characteristically, "do not take it, unless you can make up your mind to bear every species of abuse and misrepresentation and the imputation of the most sordid and interested motives." Himself, both at home and in the lobbies of the House, he consorted more and more with the Canningites. Huskisson, who followed Canning into the Government, was always coming down to Brocket. He combined profound knowledge of practical affairs with an antipathy to doctrinaire theory. This exactly harmonized with William's own point of view. His previous respect for Huskisson's judgment grew to unbounded admiration. "The greatest *practical* statesman I ever knew," he said of him in later years; and he set himself to learn all he could from such a wellspring of wisdom. Practical knowledge had always been the weakest part of William's intellectual equipment. The instruction acquired from Huskisson was to be of great service to him. Meanwhile in Parliament he steadily gave Canning such support as was possible from Whig benches. Apart from the fact that he agreed with him, he thought it important that Tory policy should be modified by more Liberal ideas, lest it should relapse into hopeless obscurantism. Since William admired him so much, it is not surprising that Canning was struck by his talents. Lamb, he declared, was unusually eloquent and able. Nor was Canning William's only admirer. During the second period of his Parliamentary life his reputation steadily increased. For all that his Canningite sympathies were by now universally recognized, he was accepted as a necessary member of the inner group of Whig leaders; when they met to talk things over at Lansdowne or Holland House, William was always asked. In Tory circles too, he was an object of approbation. Lord Castlereagh was heard to say that "William Lamb could do anything if he shook off carelessness, and set about it"; while George IV, expatiating over the wine at Windsor Castle, went so far as to prophesy that William would one day be Prime Minister.

Such tributes were extremely gratifying. But they did not give much cause for encouragement. To be Prime Minister, to be a Minister of any kind, William required a party with which he could associate himself. And the prospect of any such party coming into power looked small indeed. The Tories seemed more safely in the saddle than ever. For the country, terrified by the ominous threat of revolution that muttered round the horizon, was more than ever suspicious of any administration likely to embark on a forward policy. And anyway the Whigs were in no condition to take office. Till they were prepared to adopt a progressive programme publicly they had no alternative to offer to the existing government. And so far from agreeing on such a policy, they were more divided than ever. The Grenvillites, now merely a fossilized remnant of eighteenth-century aristocratic domination, were against all reform. The Foxites, at heart nervous of change, said they must wait till the respectable classes of the community showed themselves anxious for it; headed by Lord Grey, they had pretty well retired from politics. The more active younger group had disintegrated into a rout of quarrelling factions. Some rushed to the extreme left; others, led by Brougham, bustled agitatedly about, now flirting with the extremists, now devising elaborate programmes of moderate change, now courting Canning's favour—all in vain effort to find some effective cry with which to rally party and country to their support. As for a Canningite Coalition, there seemed little chance of that. The Government was mainly composed of diehard Tories like Lord Eldon and the Duke of Wellington. And they felt themselves too strong to need to concede anything to the more liberalizing elements in public life.

What was poor William to do? With an ironical smile and a despondent heart, he did as little as he could. Frustration and disappointment found expression in a prevailing mood of inertia. He was lax in his attendance at the House; when he was there he seldom made a speech. It was pleasanter and more profitable to stay at Brocket looking through old family letters, walking out with a gun after duck, and reading Sophocles in the library. As the years passed and no prospect of political influence appeared, his indolence grew stronger. Hope deferred maketh the heart lazy. He now sat for the local borough of Hertford: by the election of 1825, he found himself almost unable to face the effort required to ingratiate himself anew with his constituency. "William," said the irritated Emily, "canvasses very idly and says constantly that it won't do; sees everything in the light of his adversaries so that he disheartens all his own friends; and yet does not make up his mind to give up, but is always shilly shally." It was thought at first that the seat would be uncontested. But suddenly the opposition put up a disreputable young rake called Duncombe, who plunged into the fray, scattering guineas on all sides, accusing William in a striking metaphor, drawn from the racecourse, of "being unsound in both forelegs," and seeking to discredit his personal character by raking up the hoary scandals of his married life. With relief William seized the opportunity to retire from the fight. In the summer of 1826 London saw him once more a man of leisure. "In very good spirits," it was noted, "at being out of things again."

It might have been expected that his frustrated energy would have found some other outlet. And in fact he did toy with the idea of literary composition. He contributed an occasional review to the *Literary Gazette*; and when in 1819 it was proposed to him to write the life of Sheridan, he accepted; began studying documents, making notes, and sketching out preliminary plans for chapters. However, within a year he had resigned the task to Tom Moore. History gives no reason. It seems likely to have been self-distrust. "I have read too much and too little," he notes in his commonplace book somewhere about this time, "so much, that it has extinguished all the original fire of my genius, and yet not enough, to furnish me with the power of writing works of mature thinking and solid instruction." Moreover, it was late for a man of his indolent temperament to set himself to learn a new profession. Politics might not be the occupation that best suited him; but he had been immersed in them for fifteen years. By now it needed the pressure of public life to make him concentrate on a given task. To keep his mind to the effort of sustained literary composition sufficiently to achieve anything like the standard required by his exacting taste, was perhaps beyond him. At all events, after giving up Sheridan's biography he attempted nothing more. The period is as barren of literary achievement as it is of political.

Meanwhile his private life pursued a grey and unprofitable course. Here indeed there had been changes. But time had made them, not William. The eighteenth century was a memory by now: and by 1826 the last of the figures which had irradiated its setting with so incomparable a splendour, had followed it into the shadow. Lady Bessborough had died suddenly in 1821, from a chill caught while travelling in Italy. Worn out by a life of tempest and disillusion, she was glad enough to quit the world; and though racked with pain, met her end with a gentle serenity, only ruffled a little by anxiety, lest her departure might distress those whom she loved. Three years before, she had been preceded to the grave by Lady Melbourne. Her end was melancholy and unlooked for. Up till 1816 her matchless vitality had shown no signs of flagging: indomitable as ever she continued to direct her household, entertain her friends, and plot her children's advancement. Then suddenly a change came. She, who had triumphed relentlessly over so many enemies, fell herself a victim to the relentless force of mortality. Miserable, horribly fat, and doped with laudanum, she lay, at last deaf to the enticements of the world, in the clutches of a fatal disease. Only on her deathbed did the clouds lift to reveal a glimmer of her old self. She summoned Emily, now launched on a career of romance as varied as her own, to her bedside; and besought her as a last request to be true—not to her husband Lord Cowper, Lady Melbourne had too much sense to expect that—but to her first and most distinguished admirer, Lord Palmerston. And with her last breath she sought to fire William with the energy needed to achieve the great position for which from childhood she had designed him. What were his feelings, as he looked on her features, fixed in the enigmatic stillness of death? What ironical epitaph, mingling love and regret and disenchantment, rose to his lips as he took a last farewell of her who had played the chief part in moulding his disillusioning destiny? . . . No expression of his thoughts is recorded at the time; probably they were of a kind best kept to himself. Only as a very old man at Brocket, he was once found, lost in meditation, before her portrait. "A remarkable woman," he murmured to himself, "a devoted mother, an excellent wife—but not chaste, not chaste."

Lady Melbourne's place in the family was taken by Emily. Her personality was less compelling than her mother's. Bewitchingly pretty in a soft dark style, she was a charming sunshiny worldling, born with an instinctive shrewdness and social accomplishment, but spontaneous and warm-hearted, moved by no fiercer ambition than to make life as pleasant as possible for herself and everyone else. As a hostess, however, she was equally successful. Panshanger, her country seat, was as famous a fashionable centre as Melbourne House had been: and life there carried on the same tradition, disorderly and elegant, brilliant and unedifying, "full," says a visitor, "of vice and agreeableness, foreigners and roués." Emily had also inherited her mother's family sense. It was natural to her to gather her brothers round her, to keep an eye on their healths, their careers, and their affairs of the heart. William, she did find a little hard to manage; he was, she complained, so lazy and undecided—besides he ate too much. But she was devoted to him, and delighted in his company. He on his side took great pleasure in her; the beauty and success of "that little devil Emily" remained, all through life, his pride and joy. Even when he was sixty-one and she fifty-three he could not forbear asking Queen Victoria if she did not think Emily was wearing "a very dashing gown." And when the Queen expressed her admiration, "she beats any of them now," he broke out, "she was always like a pale rose." After his mother died, he spent much of his time at Panshanger:

213

lounging, arguing and being late for meals, as in a second home.

He needed one. There was little domestic amenity to be enjoyed at his own house. *Glenarvon* and Lady Heathcote's ball between them had done for Caroline. Admiration had grown to be as necessary to her as air; nothing had any interest to her except in so far as it helped her to make an impression on other people. The fact that she was now an outcast dependent solely on solitary and impersonal interests for her satisfaction meant that the backbone of her life was broken. There was nothing for her to do but disintegrate into oblivion.

Alas, it was a slow and painful process. For she was too vital to accept defeat. Instead, with the fitful energy of despair, she cast about for any means by which she might once more compel the attention and applause of mankind. Like an actress who has outlived her popularity, she continued, with unquenchable hope, again and again to try her luck before the footlights. Sometimes she appeared as a woman of intellect. During this period she published two novels and a number of poems, notably one to her husband which opened with the surprising couplet

> "Oh, I adore thee, William Lamb,
> But hate to hear thee say God damn."

She also presented herself to the public as a sportswoman. At the time of George IV's coronation she wrote offering her services as riding master to the official champion, whose task it was to ride into Westminster Hall, and fling down a challenge to anyone who might dispute the King's right to his throne. At home, Caroline sought to make an impression by playing the more modest role of efficient housewife. Fashionable visitors to Brighton one spring were astonished to see Lady Caroline Lamb on horseback in the public street spiritedly haggling with the grocer about the price of cheese: her table at Brocket was piled with elaborately worked-out schemes for the economical regulation of her household. The elections of 1819 gave her a chance to blossom forth in yet another character, that of political woman. George Lamb was standing for Westminster; and Caroline, though protesting that she was at death's door, at once drove up to London and invaded the local taverns, where she diced and drank with the voters in order to win them to the good cause. One day driving through the streets in her carriage, she was assaulted with a volley of stones by a mob of angry opponents. Here was an opportunity indeed for a heroine to display her quality. Stepping out with head held high, "I am not afraid of you," cried Caroline magnificently, "I know you will not hurt a woman—for you are Englishmen!"

In other moods she studied less to discover effective roles, than to collect an appreciative audience. Within a few months of the publication of *Glenarvon* we find her inviting her cousin Harriet Granville to pay her a visit of reconciliation at Melbourne House. "I went yesterday to Whitehall," writes Harriet, "and followed the page through the dark and winding passages and staircases. I was received with rapturous joy, embraces and tremendous spirits. I expected she would put on an appearance of something, but to do her justice she only displayed a total want of shame and consummate impudence, which whatever they may be in themselves are at least better or rather less disgusting than pretending or acting a more interesting part. I was dragged to the unresisting William and dismissed with a repetition of embrassades and professions. And this is the guilty broken-hearted Calantha who could only expiate her crimes with her death!"

In later years Caroline made sporadic attempts to recover her place in London society; wrote beseeching the Duke of Wellington to use his influence to get her readmitted to Almack's, suddenly sent out invitations for an evening party at Brocket. But for the most part she fought shy of her old friends. And, like many other people who have failed to obtain a footing in fashionable society, she fell back on the intellectual. It was not the great world that was deserting her, so she put it to herself, it was she who was leaving the great world, in pursuit of the higher satisfactions of the spirit. Accordingly, she made friends with Godwin, the philosopher, with Lady Morgan, the novelist, and Miss Benger, the historian: and was to be found, an exotic figure, at little reunions up three pairs of stairs, where, refreshed by cups of tea carried in by the solitary maidservant, the genteel intelligentsia of the Metropolis discoursed to one another on Truth and Beauty. In return she took the opportunity to display herself in the agreeable character of fairy godmother; showered her new friends with unexpected gifts of fruit and opera tickets, and invited them to Melbourne House. There on her sofa she would lie, swathed in becoming folds of muslin and surrounded by souvenirs of Lord Byron, talking by the hour of the great people she had known, and the ardours and endurances of her life of passion.

Sometimes she asked her new friends to meet her old. There is a comical account of a dinner she gave in 1820 consisting of a number of artists and writers—notably William Blake and Sir Thomas Lawrence—some humble country acquaintances and a few persons of ton, whom she had managed to entice into her house. It was not a success. Naïve Blake, it is true, was happy enough. "There is a great deal of kindness in that lady," he said looking at Caroline. But the ambitious Lawrence was not at all pleased at being seen by his fashionable patrons in such dingy-looking company: while the grandees, after taking one look at the extraordinary people they had been asked to meet, relapsed into disgusted silence. Caroline herself added to the general awkwardness by commenting loudly and unfavourably on the rest of her guests, to whichever one of them she happened to be talking.

Friends, however, had never been enough for her; to be a queen of hearts remained her most cherished aspiration; and she snatched at the slightest chance of a love affair. They were not glorious chances. She was now too notorious and eccentric to attract anyone much worth attracting. The wife of William Lamb, the lover of Byron, had to make do with hardened roués, ready to take up with any woman, or callow youths, glad to have their names connected with so celebrated a personality. However, beggars cannot be choosers. And Caroline set all her powers to the task of making the best of a bad job; represented the most trivial intrigue to herself as a passionate romantic drama; and threw herself into it with an extravagance of melodramatic gesture all the more preposterous by contrast with the ignominious unreality of the emotions involved. Every few months saw the repetition in caricature of the Byron love-affair. The old limelight was switched on: the old tricks played out: she swooned, she rhapsodized, she pounded the organ all night; she made scenes of jealousy and scenes of reconciliation. Each lover, during the period of his reign, was awarded the privilege of wearing a ring, given her by Byron. For the most presentable of her conquests, the twenty-one year old Bulwer Lytton, she even staged a death scene, summoning him to her bedside, where with pathetic faltering accents she sought to move him by a last declaration of love.

Such exhibitions could not be kept secret. Caroline did not wish them to be; besides, the sort of men she was now entangled with liked to brag of their conquest. By 1821 her reputation had sunk so low that she was suspected of an intrigue with any man she was seen with, down to her son's tutor and the family doctor, Mr. Walker. One of her stockings, so ran scandalous rumour, had been found at the end of Mr. Walker's bed. This seems to have been a libel; but London society was only too pleased to accept any evidence justifying their hostility towards her. While the Lamb family believed everything against her, and were proportionately disgusted. "It is such a low-lived thing to take a Scotch doctor for a lover," commented Emily viciously.

Nor did her affairs afford Caroline herself much compensating satisfaction. The old romantic properties were grown dreadfully faded by this time; in the hands of inferior players, the Byronic drama showed fustian indeed. She pursued her quarries with the effrontery of desperation. But try as she might she could not recapture the thrill of the past; and she quickly tired of the chase. Within a short time she dropped it; and, restless and disappointed, turned in search of some new victim to persecute with her feverish attentions.

But indeed, poor Caroline, any effort she made to mend her broken life ended equally in disaster. Each new part she appeared in was a failure. Her later novels made no hit: the Coronation champion preferred to employ a more conventional instructor: and her electioneering vagaries merely made her the laughing-stock of London. Her housewifely activities were also unsuccessful—"What is the use of saving on the one hand, if you squander all away on the other?" exclaimed William in despair. While the only effect of her intricate domestic schemes was to make the servants leave. "The servants at Brocket," says Emily, "still continue to pass through, like figures in a magic lantern. A new cook, whom Haggard * was delighted to secure from her great character and fifty guineas wages, stopped only a week. . . . Haggard, talking of Caroline, is so good. He says she cannot get any worse, so one hopes she may get better."

Caroline did not succeed in making friends either. The

* The agent at Brocket.

beau monde had done with her for good. Emily, out of
affection for William, got her re-admitted to Almack's:
but the doors of the great houses remained closed. As
for her evening-party at Brocket, it was a fiasco. The
rooms shone with a galaxy of candles; the tables were
spread with supper for eighty people; Caroline sent her
own carriage to fetch those guests who lived far off. But
only ten people came. Her excursions into other social
spheres were less openly disastrous. Then, as always, the
intelligentsia were susceptible to the charms of rank and
fashion; while Caroline was delighted at first to find
people who gazed at her with awe, and believed every
word she said. All the same there was a gulf between
them and her that no amount of snobbery on their part,
or vanity on hers, could overspan. Serious, stiff and
middle class, they were bewildered alike by the splendour
of her surroundings, the candour of her confidences and
the modish effusiveness of her manners. She was equally
at sea with them. That Lady Morgan should not be able
to afford to keep a groom of the chambers!—Caroline
had not imagined that such sordid poverty was possible.
And she consternated Miss Benger, by suddenly bursting
in on her one morning, while she was occupied in the
plebeian task of counting the washing. Poor Miss Benger!
she thought she would die of shame when Lady Caroline's dog pulled out a heap of dirty handkerchiefs and

stockings from under the sofa, where she had hastily shoved them on the arrival of her distinguished visitor. Moreover, after the first fun of impressing them was over, Caroline was bored with her new friends. Intellectual persons for the most part are less socially accomplished than fashionable ones; their conversation may have more stuff in it, but it is not so graceful. Caroline, accustomed to Devonshire House, grew conscious of this. "These sort of people," she confided to a friend, "are not always agreeable, but vulgar, quaint and formal. Still I feel indebted to them, for they have one and all treated me with kindness . . . when I was turned out." In plain words she only associated with them, because those she liked better would have nothing to do with her. It was the devastating truth, and she recognized it.

For this was the most distressing feature of her predicament. She realized her failures even though she refused to accept them. Her natural acuteness was always at war with her power of self-deception. Though she could persuade herself of anything, it was never for long. In consequence, the logic of facts forced her gradually, reluctantly, agonizingly, to relinquish her illusions; step by step she found herself compelled to recognize that her literary powers were small, that the intelligentsia bored her, that her lovers were a poor lot. At last she actually admitted that her misfortunes were mainly her own fault.

Even then it was impossible for her to regard herself in an unsympathetic light. And she fell back on a last desperate pose of pitiful victim; a fragile butterfly, worthless and shallow perhaps, but punished far beyond her deserts by the harsh decrees of destiny. "I am like the wreck of a little boat," she wrote to Godwin, "for I never come up to the sublime and beautiful—merely a little gay merry boat which perhaps stranded itself at Vauxhall or London Bridge; or wounded without killing itself, as a butterfly does in a tallow candle. There is nothing marked sentimental or interesting in my career; all I know is that I was happy, well, rich, surrounded by friends. I have now one faithful friend in William Lamb, two more in my father, brother, but health, spirits and all else is gone—gone how? O assuredly not by the visitation of God but slowly gradually by my own fault." And again, "It were all very well one died at the end of a tragic scene, after playing a desperate part, but if one lives and instead of growing wiser remains the same victim of every folly and passion, without the excuse of youth and inexperience what then? There is no particular reason I should exist, it conduces to no one's happiness and on the contrary I stand in the way of many. Besides I seem to have lived a thousand years and feel I am neither wiser, better nor worse than when I began . . . this is probably the case of millions but that does not mend the matter; and while a fly exists, it seeks to save itself." The appropriate end of such a character was clearly to die. And, in order to squeeze the last tear of pity from her audience, Caroline now took every few weeks or so to announcing her speedily approaching death.

In 1821 the spectre of her tumultuous past rose, in a succession of dramatic events, to trouble her distracted spirit still further. "I was taken ill in March," she told a friend, "in the middle of the night, I fancied I saw Lord Byron—I screamed, jumped out of bed . . . he looked horrible, and ground his teeth at me, he did not speak; his hair was straight; he was fatter than when I knew him and not near so handsome. . . . I am glad to think that it occurred before his death, as I never did and hope I never shall see a ghost. I even avoided enquiring about the exact day for fear I should believe it—it made enough impression as it was. . . . Judge what my horror was as well as grief when long after, the news came of his death; it was conveyed to me in two or three words—'Caroline behave properly, I know it will shock you, Lord Byron is dead.' This letter I received, when laughing at Brocket Hall."

As a consequence she took to her bed with a serious attack of hysterical fever. Three months later when she was just beginning to recover, she went out driving. As her carriage emerged through the park gates it was met by a funeral cortege, grim with all the murky pageantry of plumes and mourning coaches, wending its way through the serene summer landscape. William, who was riding beside her, trotted on to ask whose it was. "Lord Byron's," was the answer. Fearful of the effect of the sudden shock on Caroline, he did not tell her at the time: but when she heard it that night, once more she collapsed.

Such a collapse was only the intensification of what was now a chronic condition. Caroline was not the woman to rise superior to misfortune. Her self-respect was broken, and under the repeated batterings of fate her character gradually went to pieces. She began to exhibit all the painful, pitiable traits of the déclassée person; thrusting herself defiantly forward when she was not wanted, yet on edge, all the time, to take offence at insults real or imagined. Blinding herself to her present situation, she talked continually of the famous people she had known, with an embarrassing and unsuccessful pretence that she was as intimate with them as ever. Meanwhile her nerves were now permanently at the same pitch of irritability as at the height of the Byron episode. Not a week passed without some dreadful scene when she sobbed and kicked and screamed insane abuse at anyone who came near her. As for breaking things, it had become a habit: it was computed on one occasion that she had destroyed £200 worth of china in a morning. Rather than face the torture of her solitary thoughts, she took to galloping frantically round the park all day, and sitting up all night, holding forth to anyone who could be persuaded to listen. When all else failed she sought oblivion in laudanum and brandy. Loss of self-respect also showed itself in the ordering of her life. Unequal to the discipline of regular meals, she had food placed about the house that she might snatch a bite when and where she felt inclined: she grew squalid and careless in her person; while her bedroom presented a curious image of moral and mental disintegration. It was decked out with every fantastic caprice of the romantic fancy. An altar cloth, a portrait of Byron, and "an elegant crucifix" hung conspicuous on the walls. But the curtains were in holes: the furniture was scattered with half-finished plates of cake and pickles. While on the dressing-table, flanked by a prayer-book on one side and on the other by a flask of lavender water, stood shamelessly the brandy bottle.

It was not an auspicious setting for domestic happiness. William's married life after 1816 was even more disagreeable than before. In a sense he was better equipped to bear it. For he entered on it with open eyes. He recognized himself as the lunatic's guardian, which in fact he was; and strove to approach his task with the firm but kindly detachment suitable to it. There was no question of his pretending, either to Caroline or to anyone else, that he thought marriage a pleasant state. One day when the family were gathered round the Brocket dinner table the conversation turned on matrimony. Caroline opined that husband and wife should live in separate houses; while William, though admitting that people had better marry, said that only the very rich could expect to be happier by so doing. "People who are forced to live together," he declared, "and are confined to the same rooms and the same bed are like two pigeons under a basket, who must fight." He was also completely hardened by now, to Caroline's making a public exhibition of herself. Emily was outraged when, at the height of the Mr. Walker scandal, she saw William at a concert in company with Caroline and her reputed lover. "William looked such a fool arriving with them," she said, "and looking as pleased as Punch, and she looking so disgusting with her white cross and dirty gown as if she had been rolled in a kennel." As a matter of fact, so far from her lovers' annoying him, he looked on them as fellow victims for whose sufferings he could feel nothing but sympathy. "William Lamb was particularly kind to me," said Bulwer Lytton after describing an appalling series of scenes with Caroline, while staying at Brocket. "I think he saw my feelings. He is a singularly fine character for a man of the world."

At the same time William still felt a responsibility towards her: and did all he could to alleviate her unhappiness. Such of her activities as seemed comparatively harmless had all his encouragement. He was always pressing Emily to try and get her asked about in London society; at Caroline's request he assisted Godwin in his career. And he took an immense amount of trouble to help her in her novels; going over every sentence with her, and himself sending the finished manuscript to the publisher with a covering letter. Consistent with his new attitude to her, he made no attempt to recommend them above their merits.

"The incongruity of, and objection to, the story of 'Ada Reis' can only be got over by power of writing, beauty of sentiment, striking and effective situation, etc. If Mr. Gifford thinks there is in the first two volumes anything of excellence sufficient to overbalance their manifest faults, I still hope that he will press upon Lady Caroline the absolute necessity of carefully reconsidering and revising the third volume, and particularly the conclusion of the novel. . . . I think, if it were thought that anything could be done with the novel, and that the fault of its design and structure can be got over, that I could put her in the way of writing up this part a little, and giving it something of strength, spirit, and novelty, and of making it at once more moral and more interesting. I wish you would communicate these my hasty suggestions to Mr. Gifford, and he will see the propriety of pressing Lady Caroline to take a little more time to this part of the novel. She will be guided by his authority, and her fault at present is to be too hasty and too impatient of the trouble of correcting and recasting what is faulty."

He also did his best to soothe her nerves. It was to William that everyone turned, if Caroline became more than usually unmanageable. One day she was making arrangements for a dinner-party at Brocket. Exasperated at what she considered the stupidity of the butler in failing to grasp her ideas of decoration, she suddenly leapt on to the dinner-table, and fixed herself in a fantastic attitude which she requested him to take as the model from which to arrange the centrepiece. The poor man, terrified by her extraordinary appearance, ran to William for help. He came immediately. "Caroline, Caroline," he said in tranquillizing tones, and gently lifting her from the table carried her from the room.

Caroline was not his only care at Brocket. He also concerned himself with his son. Augustus was now in his teens; but mentally he remained a child of seven. A strong well-grown boy, he caused dismay by romping half-dressed into the drawing-room when the housekeeper was setting it to rights, tumbling her over and sitting on her. But William never faced the fact that his deficiency was incurable. Despairing of his wife, he clung all the more desperately to the hope that something might be made of his child. No stone was left unturned; he consulted every kind of doctor and psychological expert, and procured a special tutor, for whom he had prepared an elaborate scheme of education, including lessons in logic, moral philosophy and metaphysics. All of course in vain; it was as much as the tutor could do to teach Augustus to read and write. But William obstinately, pathetically, refused to despair.

About Caroline he showed less fortitude. In spite of all his resolution he was unable to make even a modified success of his relationship with her. For he was in a false position. It was all very well to try and behave as the guardian of a lunatic. But William had neither the taste nor the talent for such a part. He had embarked on it mainly from weakness; because he could not face the unpleasantness of breaking with her. In consequence he was not supported in his ordeal by any conviction that he was doing right. And he could not stand the strain. As the years went by his patience progressively crumbled.

He went away from Brocket as often as he could. During the time he spent there, he lived in a state of nervous tension, morbidly apprehensive of an outburst; when it came, he flew out into a violent passion; and then in the end gave way to her completely for the sake of peace. Such a situation could not last. By 1825 William at last admitted he had made a mistake in trying to settle down with her again. Once more he decided on a separation.

The process of its accomplishment was a caricature of all the least admirable features in their relationship. Never had he been weaker or she more intolerable. He was still too frightened to face breaking the news to her in person; so in March he went off to Brighton, where he wrote to her saying he was never coming back. This provoked the storm that might have been expected. However, by May her letters had grown so much calmer that he decided to go down to Brocket to discuss the necessary arrangements. It was a mad risk to take. To begin with Caroline was all right; quiet, sensible, and at moments so entertaining that she kept William in fits of laughter. But, when he began to talk business, the other Caroline appeared. She wanted an allowance of £3,000 a year: he, though his family offered to help him, could not see his way to giving her more than the £2,000 on which they had lived up till then. In the twinkling of an eye she had become a fury, "relapsed," he said bitterly, "into

231

her usual course of abuse, invective and the most unrestrained violence." She wrote round to her relations alleging that he beat her; and accusing him in the same breath of ruining her character by over-indulgence and driving her to desperation by his cruelty. She was the more unbridled, because for once she had a supporter. Her brother, William Ponsonby, "reckoned an ass and a jackanapes by everybody," said Emily tartly, was sufficiently convinced by Caroline's reports to write off to William in the strain of Lady Catherine de Bourgh; saying that he could not allow his sister to be trampled on by William, who owed her a great deal for deigning to marry someone of such inferior social position. Not trusting himself to answer such a communication with discretion, William went away and left the affair in Emily's hands. She, to use her own words, "bullied the bully" by telling Caroline that rather than give way William would take the whole thing into court. Caroline was always ready for publicity, even of an undesirable kind: but her relations were more reasonable. In the end the matter was referred to the arbitration of her cousins Lord Althorp and the Duke of Devonshire, who proposed a compromise of £2,500 a year. Both parties accepted the settlement; neither was pleased with it. William thought he would never be able to afford so large a sum; Caroline, on the other hand, informed her friends that she was going to be so poor, as to be in danger of dying of starvation. Indeed the version of this particular passage in her history, which she published to the world, had even less relation to the truth than usual. At the same time that she was squabbling with William over money and accusing him of every vice under heaven, she told Lady Morgan that she loved him more than anyone in the world, and that he was being forced away from her against his will by the machinations of his family. Her letter ended with the usual announcement of her imminent demise. "If I would but sign a paper," she said, with bitter sarcasm, "all my rich relations will protect me, and I shall no doubt go with an Almack's ticket to heaven."

Trouble was not yet at an end. It was one thing to persuade Caroline to sign; it was another to get her out of the house. She refused to move till she had decided what to do. "Shall I go abroad?" she asks Lady Morgan. "Shall I throw myself upon those who no longer want me, or shall I live a good sort of half kind of life in some cheap street a little way off, the City Road, Shoreditch, Camberwell or upon the top of a shop—or shall I give lectures to little children, and keep a seminary and thus earn my bread? Or shall I write a kind of quiet everyday sort of novel full of wholesome truths, or shall I attempt to be poetical, and failing beg my friends for a guinea a-piece, and their name, to sell my work upon

233

the best foolscap paper; or shall I fret, fret and die; or shall I be dignified and fancy myself as Richard the Second did when he picked the nettle up—upon a thorn?"

Faced with such variety of sensational alternatives to choose from, there seemed no reason she should ever make up her mind. And William, exhausted by the unnatural energy of purpose he had exerted during the first part of the year, now reacted into a listless indolence, in which he refused to put any pressure on her. On the contrary, to his family's irritation, he was always paying her visits in order to keep her in a good humour. At last in August Caroline decided that she wanted to go to Paris. A tremendous farewell scene was staged at Brocket, in which Caroline played her part so affectingly that even the butler—so she noted with satisfaction—was bathed in tears. By the 14th she was over the Channel. It was a very bad crossing: "She will, I trust," writes Emily, "have been so sick as to feel little anxiety to cross the water again directly."

This pious hope proved vain. Within two months her relations-in-law were dismayed to learn that Caroline had reappeared at an inn in Dover; whence she wrote to all and sundry giving a heart-rending picture of the poverty-stricken state to which she was reduced; "in a little dreary apartment," made drearier by the peals of heartless laughter that rose from the neighbouring smoking-room, destitute, she complained, of such necessities of life as pages, carriages, horses and fine rooms; and accusing the Lambs, with a wild disregard for truth, of conspiring with her doctor to say that she was mad, in order that they might withhold from her her meagre allowance. "William," she asserted, "is enchanted at the prospect of giving me nothing." The plain fact was that she was far too unbalanced to be able to manage life on her own. And there was no knowing the trouble in which she would involve herself and everyone else, unless she was looked after. Since no one else offered, the Lambs reluctantly took on the task again. Just three months after taking a last farewell of Brocket, she was settled there once more. William, clinging to the outward form of separation, still had his official home in London. But since he felt himself obliged to pay her frequent visits in order to see how she was getting on, his situation, with regard to her, was not essentially altered. It seemed as if, in personal life as in public, all his efforts to free himself ended equally in frustration.

In reality, however, the long drawn-out drama was near its close. Unknown alike to William and to Caroline, the fates had decided to cut the coil which for so many years had bound them, one to another, in wretched conjunction. The ordeal of the separation marked an epoch in Caroline's life. For the agitations it involved

had put a fatal final strain on her already worn-out constitution. At last her amazing vitality began to ebb.
From this time on, in a dying fall, a strange muted tranquillity, her storm-tossed career declined swiftly to its
period. Once, during the first few months after her return to Brocket, a glimpse of the old Caroline showed
itself. Bulwer had become engaged to a Miss Wheeler.
And Caroline, partly from pique at his fickleness, partly
because she saw the theatrical possibilities inherent in the
situation, invited Miss Wheeler to Brocket, where she
staged a little scene: Caroline, an experienced woman of
the world, with kindly wisdom warns Miss Wheeler, an
innocent girl, against the perfidy of men. "Don't let Edward Bulwer let you down," she adjured her ominously,
"They are a bad set." This piece of sentimental comedy,
however, was a faint echo indeed of the thundering melo-
dramas of Caroline's prime. And it was the last echo.
After this her days passed in eventless rural monotony.
"How can I write," she tells a friend, "even imagination
must have some material on which to work. I have
none. Passion might produce sentiment of some sort.
But mine are all calmed or extinct. . . . Memory—a
waste with nothing in it worth recording! Happy,
healthy, contented, quiet, I get up at half past four, ride
about with Hazard, see harvesters at work in the pretty
green confined country; read a few old books, see no one,

hear from no one." No longer did her spirit leap out at the call of fame; no longer did she combat hostile fate in baffled rage, or seek to forget it in the brandy bottle. Instead, profoundly weary, she lay back clinging to the comfort of safe homely innocent things, conscious only of a numbed longing to be at peace. So great a change in the direction of her desires brought with it an equal change in her character. The fury of her egotism dwindled with the vitality of which it was the expression. A child always, she was now a tired child, gentle and submissive, pathetically terrified of annoying people, stretching out her arms to be soothed and cherished. Frederick and Emily, driving over from Panshanger to pay her a visit, found all their age-old hostility towards her melting away: Caroline appeared so sincerely, so touchingly anxious to behave as they wanted. Still more did she want to behave as William wanted. For, as the fever of her maturity left her, so also did the memory of its preoccupations. Bulwer, Webster, Byron himself were as though they had never been: and the old first love, fresh and single as in honeymoon days, brimmed back into her heart. By this time William's life had begun to change; in August, 1827, he was given an official appointment in Ireland. While he was there she wrote to him continually, naïve careful letters, asking him assiduously about his life, detailing the little facts of hers, and without

237

a word about her own feelings. Alas, he had suffered too deeply at her hands to be able to respond with the same ardour. She had broken something in him that could never be mended. But when he saw the change in her, a generous tenderness welled up in his spirit that washed away any trace of bitterness that might lurk there. He answered her letters with affectionate kindness, saved up such scraps of news as he thought might entertain her, encouraged any plan of hers that seemed likely to give her pleasure.

"My dear Caroline," runs a typical letter, "I am very much obliged to you for your letters—and much pleased with them—I never knew you more rational or quiet, and you say nothing which doesn't give me great pleasure—Matters are a little uncertain in the political world, but at any rate I think a tour to Paris would do you good, provided you can avoid making scamps of acquaintance, which is your great fault and danger—I went down to dine at Bellevue; where I saw Mr. Peter La Touche, 94 years old past—he dined with us. Mrs. La Touche had tried to persuade him not, but he was determined upon it. They keep him on a strict regimen of sherry and water, but if he can get at a bottle of wine now he drinks it off in a crack—there is a fine old cod for you." . . .

TEN YEARS LATER

It is significant of the strength of the bond that bound him to her, that now Caroline was no longer provoking him, he began at once to try and excuse her to himself on the old plea. Other people, not she, were responsible for her errors: Let her avoid making friends with scamps, and he was only too anxious for her to go herself to Paris or anywhere else if she fancied it might make her happy. But there was to be no more travelling for her in this world. As the year advanced, her health began to exhibit alarming symptoms. In October, 1827, the doctors reported her to be dangerously ill of dropsy. From the first Caroline was sure her case was hopeless. But the conviction did not disperse her calm. On the contrary, her spirit rose to meet its stern ordeal; and, face to face with death, that streak of genuine nobility, which a lifetime of folly had not succeeded in wholly eradicating from her nature, showed itself as never before. She did not, indeed, give up dramatizing herself; she would not have been Caroline if she had. Appreciating to the full the pathos of her situation, she rallied all her strength in the effort to stage a death scene which should do her credit. Still, there is something heroic in a sense of the stage that is unquelled by the presence of death itself; and moreover the role, in which Caroline chose to make her last appearance before the world, was for once worthy of the heroine she had so long aspired to be. She showed no fear; she sought refuge neither in self-deception nor self-pity. Though racked with suffering, she lay hour by hour through the darkening autumn days, quiet and unmurmuring; her chief concern to convince others, in the short time that remained to her, how sorry she was for the needless suffering she had brought on them. "Dearest Maria," she writes to Lady Duncannon, her eldest brother's wife, "as I cannot sit up, I am obliged to use a pencil. . . . I consider my painful illness as a great blessing—I feel returned to my God and duty and my dearest husband: and my heart which was so proud and insensible is quite overcome with the great kindness I receive—I have brought myself to be quite another person and broke that hard spell which prevented me saying my prayers; so that if I were better, I would go with you and your dear children to church. I say all this, dearest Maria, lest you should think I flew to Religion because I was in danger—it is no such thing, my heart is softened, I see how good and kind others are, and I am quite resigned to die. I do not myself think there is a chance for me." And to Lady Morgan, with a flash of her old bewitching whimsicality, she says, "I am on my death-bed: say I might have died by a diamond, I die now by a brickbat: but remember the only noble fellow I ever met with is William Lamb. He is to me what Shore was to Jane Shore." For, now at this final crisis of her troubled history, it was William who more than ever filled her thoughts. His name was always on her lips; she still wrote to him regularly and with no word of complaint— she who was used to complain so often and so groundlessly —and she besought the doctors not to tell him of her condition lest it might be a worry to him. There was no concealing it however. Lady Morgan, visiting Ireland, saw him one evening sunk in black depression at the news. A day or two later, he sent her the doctor's report with a covering note. "It is with great pain I send you the enclosed. It is some consolation that she is now relieved from pain: but illness is a terrible thing." To Caroline herself, when she rallied a little, he wrote with an emotion all the more poignant for the reserve with which it is expressed. "My dear C, I received your little line yesterday; and later received with great pleasure Dr. Goddard's account that you were a little better. My heart is almost broken that I cannot come over directly: but your brother, to whom I have written, will explain to you the difficult situation in which I am placed. How unfortunate and melancholy that you should be so ill now, and that it should be at a time when I, who have had so many years of idleness, am so fixed and held down by circumstances."

His ordeal was not to be protracted. In December Caroline, now removed by medical advice to London, was visibly sinking. It was noticed that she spoke with diffi-culty and that she seemed unable to take in what was going on round her. By the middle of January, it be-came clear that the end was near. Then only "Send for William," she whispered with a last effort of her spent forces, "he is the only person who has never failed me." He did not fail her now. Within a few days he had arrived at Melbourne House. And alone behind closed doors, they spoke to one another for the last time. It was for this only she had waited. A day or two later, her sister-in-law, Mrs. George Lamb, watching by her still form, heard a little sigh. She looked more closely: Caro-line was dead.

William was out of the room at the time. When he was told the news he was sunk for a day or two in grief. Then, to all appearance his usual self, he went back to work. But this was no sign of insensibility. Sad experi-ence had taught him that no purpose is served by unavail-ing lamentation: "solitude and retirement cherish grief," he once wrote to a bereaved friend, "employment and ex-ertion are the only means of dissipating it." In reality Caroline's death affected him profoundly. Detached from her as he had learnt to make himself, painful and frustrated as his feeling towards her had grown to be, it yet remained different in kind from what he felt towards anyone else. "In spite of all," he was to say in later days, "she was more to me than anyone ever was, or ever will be." For years afterward the mere mention of her name brought tears into his eyes; and plunged him into melancholy reverie. "Shall we meet?" he would be heard murmuring to himself, "shall we meet in another world?"

B UT THIS is to anticipate. In 1826 William's life was still at a standstill. So far as outward circumstances were concerned, it was unchanged since 1816. All the same these ten years had not been unimportant in his history. Frustrated of active outlet, his energies concentrated themselves on the development of his inner man. It was high time. For though he had been a precocious youth, at about twenty-six he had begun to mark time. The perturbations of his marriage, the preoccupations of his social and political life, required so much of his vitality as to leave little over for the maturing of mind and personality. Besides he was the sort of character that, in any circumstances, does not come of age till middle life. His nature was composed of such diverse elements that it took a long time to fuse them into a stable whole. Certainly he needed some slow blank period in which to digest his experience. These ten years were a bit of luck for him, whether he realized it or not.

In the first place they gave his intelligence space to develop. During this period he read omnivorously. No more than at Cambridge was it an orderly sort of reading. From Pindar to Shakespeare, from Thucydides to St. Augustine, from French to Latin, from philosophy to novels, he turned as the fancy took him. But the very diversity of his fancy meant that he covered a great deal of ground. And if his reading was unsystematic, it was the very opposite of superficial. He pondered, he compared, he memorized; the Elizabethan drama, for instance, he knew so well that he could repeat by heart whole scenes not only of Shakespeare but of Massinger; the margins of his books were black with the markings of his flowing illegible hand. He educated himself outside the library as well. When he was shooting—he loved the sport and was often out six hours a day—he took the opportunity to observe the habits of the wild creatures and note them down. On a landlord's ride round his father's property he would pick up information about agriculture, committing it to his memory for future reference. And he thought as much as he observed. More, in fact; for, to

William, information was only interesting in so far as it illustrated a universal law. It was the nature of his mind to argue from the particular to the general; and he kept a commonplace book, in which he noted down the generalizations that were always springing to his mind. Sometimes they were the fruit of his reading:

"Never disregard a book because the author of it is a foolish fellow."

"A curious book might be made of the great actions performed by actors whose names had not been preserved, the glories of the anonymous."

We find him speculating as to why it is, that the spirit of a past period, so vivid in an original document, evaporates completely in the process of translation; or comparing the attitude of the Greeks to Alcibiades, with that of the English to Fox. He made it a rule, if a passage in a book started a train of thought in his mind, to pursue it to its conclusion, and then jot this down before he forgot it. At other times his reflections are the product of his personal experience. He had seen a great deal of human nature in his time. Now he began to meditate on it. Why did people get married? How did they manage their incomes? What was the secret of their success or failure?

246

THE FINISHED PRODUCT

What fundamentally are the prevailing forces in public and private life? The pages of his book are littered with questionings and generalizations on these subjects. As time passed the different aspects of his thought began to connect themselves one with another; the wisdom he had acquired from books, to relate itself to the wisdom he had acquired from life. Gradually his scattered reflections composed themselves into a philosophy, his unconsciously acquired point of view built up for itself a conscious intellectual basis and justification.

Along with this mental development, went a development of character. The lessons of experience sank in and began to modify his native disposition; insensibly he began to control such impulses in himself as were inconsistent with what he believed, to give rein to those that his intelligence approved. Time, too, did its work on him; stripping his nature of such characteristics as were merely youthful and superficial, sharpening and stabilizing those that were of its essence. Slowly, the difficult process of maturity accomplished itself; bit by bit William's temperament and his intelligence, the influence of his heredity and his education, of his married life, his social life, and his public life, integrated themselves into a completed personality. At forty-seven he was at last, the William Lamb, Lord Melbourne, of later days. As it is in this character that he cuts a figure in English history, it may be permitted to us to pause for a moment, and examine it in greater detail.

To look at he was extremely prepossessing, "handsome, verging to portly," said an observer, "with a sweet countenance and an expression of refined, easy, careless good humour. He was too well-bred to seem unpleasantly sensual; but his whole person, expression and manner showed a pleasure-loving nature, indulgent to himself and to others." Indeed, age, while abating little of the sparkle of his youthful good looks, had enriched them with a new mellowness. His well-cut countenance radiated the comfortable glow that comes from years of good living; beneath his thick greying brows the eyes gleamed out, brilliant as ever, but with an added softness of geniality. His demeanour was of a piece with his appearance. There is no more talk of his arrogance or self-consciousness. Natural talent had united with long experience to make him the perfect man of the world, whose manners, at once unobtrusive and accomplished, could handle the most delicate situation with light-handed mastery, and shed round every conversation an atmosphere of delightful ease. Yet there was nothing studied about him. On the contrary, the first thing that struck most people meeting him was that he was surprisingly, eccentrically natural. Abrupt and casual, he seemed to saunter through

WILLIAM LAMB in middle-life
*From a water colour sketch in the possession of
the Lady Desborough*

life, swearing when he pleased, laughing when he pleased
—with an odd infectious explosive "ha, ha!"—sprawling
about in chairs, taking his meals with unashamed relish,
and jerking out anything apparently that came into his
head. It was his frankness that, above all, astonished.
On the most dignified occasions, solemn political councils,
stiff social gatherings, when everybody else was guarded
or stilted, William Lamb talked exactly as if he were at
home; came out, in lazy flippant colloquial tones, with
some candid comment that made the whole pompous
pretence immediately ridiculous.

His habits were equally unconventional. He was full
of queer idiosyncrasies of behaviour: gleeful rubbing together of his hands if he were amused, odd ejaculations,
"eh, eh" before he made a remark; and, a curious gesture,
passing a finger to the back of his head while he was talking. His letters were folded and sealed anyhow; the
pockets of his beautifully-cut coats bulged with a confusion of papers and bank notes; he never could be both-
ered with a watch, but would just shout to a passing
servant to tell him the time; he went to sleep when and
wherever the mood took him; in a fit of absent-minded-
ness he would start talking to himself in the midst of a
company of strangers. Indeed, though they liked him,
people found him perplexing in more ways than one.
Here we come to his third salient characteristic. He was

mysterious. It was partly that, for all his apparent frankness, he was discreet. Persons coming away from an interview with him, in which he had seemed to talk with
complete candour, would suddenly realize that he had not
given himself away on any point that really mattered. On
the contrary they wondered nervously if they had not
given themselves away to him. His air of idle nonchalance lulled them at first into thinking he noticed little.
But then, looking up at him by chance, they would perceive, darting out beneath the half-closed lids, a keen
glance that seemed to penetrate to their very hearts.

But most of all his point of view baffled them. His
conversation was fascinating; the fine flower of Whig
agreeability, at once light and learned, civilized and spontaneous, but made individual by the play of his whimsical
fancy and the gusto of his good spirits—"There was a glee
in his mirth," it was remarked, "indescribably charming."
But the spirit, the intention behind the discourse—ah, that
was elusive. Was William Lamb serious? Certainly he
sometimes seemed to be. He would talk ardently on the
most solemn subjects, political principle, the doctrines of
Christianity. Yet within a few minutes he was conversing with equal animation in a different and less edifying
strain. He had the typical eighteenth-century enjoyment
of animal humour; "Now," he would say with zest as the
dining-room doors shut on the ladies, leaving the gentle-

men to their wine, "now we can talk broad." And even on serious subjects his tone was ambiguous. Its salient characteristic was irony, a mischievous, enigmatic irony, that played audaciously over the most sacred topics, leaving its hearer very much in doubt whether William Lamb thought them sacred at all. Paradox, too, was of the fibre of his talk. He loved to defend the indefensible. "What I like about the Order of the Garter," he once remarked, "is that there is no damned merit about it." Much as he appreciated poetry, he professed to welcome the news of a poet's death. "It is a good thing when these authors die," he confided, "for then one gets their works, and is done with them." His paradoxes grew bolder, the more astonishment they created. If he was talking to anyone who struck him as a prig or a humbug, they would pile themselves wickedly one on the other, till his bewildered interlocutor relapsed into shocked silence. Indeed, William's whole personality was a paradox. Racy and refined, sensible and eccentric, cynical and full of sentiment, direct and secretive, each successive impression he made seemed to contradict the last.

Yet each impression was a true one. The outward paradox mirrored accurately the paradox within. His new mildness of demeanour, for example, was no pretence. As with age he grew more independent of other people's opinions, native fastidiousness began to modify

family custom. The Lamb robustness remained, but refined into a charming brusquerie. Experience, too, had
softened him. It is the proof of his essential fineness of
disposition, that he profited by suffering. The difficulties
of his private, the disappointments of his public life, so
far from hardening him, had taught him to be tolerant in
practice as well as in theory. Further, the unsatisfactory
spectacle of his own career disposed him to look kindly
on the shortcomings of others. Profoundly unegotistic,
he judged the rest of the world as he would judge himself.

But he was not at one with himself. On the contrary,
maturity had only intensified the discord within him. His
intellectual judgment was more cynically realistic than
ever. All he had seen of the world confirmed him in his
view that it was ruled mainly by folly, vanity, and selfishness. This is the burden of almost every observation on
human nature in his notebook:

> "Your friends praise your abilities to the skies, submit
> to you in argument, and seem to have the greatest
> deference for you; but, though they may ask it, you
> never find them following your advice upon their own
> affairs; nor allowing you to manage your own, with-
> out thinking that you should follow theirs. Thus, in
> fact, they all think themselves wiser than you, whatever
> they may say."

THE FINISHED PRODUCT

"It wounds a man less to confess that he has failed in any pursuit through idleness, neglect, the love of pleasure, etc., etc., which are his own faults, than through incapacity and unfitness, which are the faults of his nature."

"Persons in general are sufficiently ready to set themselves off by communicating their knowledge, but they are not so willing to communicate their ignorance. They are apt, both in writing and conversation, to stop when they come to the precise difficulty of the subject, which they are unable to get over, with such common phrases as 'it were easy to push these considerations much further,' or 'with the rest you are perfectly well acquainted.'"

"When a man is determined by his own inclination either to act or not to act in a particular manner, he invariably sets about devising an argument by which he may justify himself to himself for the line he is about to pursue."

"If you make an estimate of your expenses for the coming year, and upon that estimate you find that they exactly amount to or fall little short of your income, you may be sure that you are an embarrassed, if not a ruined man."

"Wealth is so much the greatest good that Fortune has to bestow that in the Latin and English languages it has usurped her name."

"You should never assume contempt for that which it is not very manifest that you have it in your power to possess, nor does a wit ever make a more contemptible figure than when, in attempting satire, he shows that he does not understand that which he would make the subject of his ridicule."

And when someone quoted to him an old observation of his own to the effect that man could only learn by experience, "No, no," he returned sadly, "nobody learns anything by experience; everybody does the same thing over and over again."

This last reflects, indirectly, as much on himself as on others. It was the measure of his detachment, that he never excepted himself from his condemnation of human beings in general. His contempt was not arrogant. This makes it more amiable; but it shows how thoroughly disillusioned he was. As for the ideal motives by which people professed to be actuated, he thought them the most fantastic illusions of all; smoke screens raised by men in order to hide from themselves the fact of their own selfishness. If, by any rare chance, idealists were sincere, it could only be because they were too stupid to understand the nature of things. "A doctrinaire," he used to say, "is a fool but an honest man." Or again, "Nobody ever did anything very foolish except from some strong principle."

Yet his heart continued to rebel against the conclusions of his reason. His sensibility was as tremblingly keen as in youth. He did not believe in human virtue: but he recognized goodness when he saw it; and he loved it. Even if public life was in fact a shoddy, self-seeking affair, how heart-stirring a pageant did it contrive to present! A moving tale still brought the tears to William's eyes, an heroic deed still fired him to a glow of generous admiration. The grace of girlhood, the sweetness of friendship, the charm of garden solitude, vain and ephemeral though they might be, set him throbbing with exquisite and poignant emotions. And now and again his spirit was touched by sublimer visitations. Suddenly there would sweep over him a mysterious sense of some august and unearthly power behind the show of things, governing human destiny. "I consider," he once broke out, unexpectedly and with emotion, to an embarrassed Cabinet meeting, "that England has been under the special protection of Divine Providence at certain periods of her history; the Spanish Armada, for instance, and the retirement of the French squadron from Bantry Bay."

And on another occasion, "I do not approve," he said, "of the condemnation in Fénelon, of those whom he is pleased to call mystics—to which persuasion I belong." Indeed these curious spiritual intimations of his were in the nature of direct mystical experience. They did not lead him to adopt a thorough-going mystical philosophy; for they came too seldom and too fleetingly for him to feel justified in founding an intellectual structure on them. Besides, he could find no logical ground for believing in their truth. But he was too sincere not to recognize their convincing reality as long as they lasted. And though they did not displace his rationalism, they undermined its security. Uneasily he hung suspended between two opinions.

No wonder he was paradoxical! What was life but a bundle of contradictions? No wonder he was ironical; faced by the preposterous incongruity of experience, the only thing a reasonable person could do was to shrug his shoulders and smile. His duality of vision appears in his attitude to every sort of subject. No one appreciated better the achievements of culture: but he did not believe they had ever seriously influenced mankind. "Raphael was employed to decorate the Vatican", he said, "not because he was a great painter but because his uncle was architect to the Pope." In politics he united a mystical patriotism and a disinterested wish to do the best for his country, to a scornful disbelief in the sacredness of any human institution, the good sense of any political ideal. Again, though his heart was so abnormally tender that he could hardly hear a tale of suffering without tears, humanitarian schemes raised in him a violent antagonism. "I am not a subscribing sort of fellow," he would reply breezily to earnest persons asking him to contribute to a philanthropic cause. Educational reformers, factory reformers—the only result of their efforts, he alleged, would be to worry the poor. As for the anti-slavery fanatics, he thought them perfectly futile. "I say, Archbishop," he once remarked to Archbishop Whateley, "what do you think I would have done about this slavery business if I had my own way? I would have done nothing at all. I would have left it all alone. It is all a pack of nonsense. There always have been slaves in most civilized countries, the Greeks, the Romans. However, they *would* have their own way and we have abolished slavery. But it is all great folly." It was their confidence in their own ability to do good that put him off humanitarians so much. Little did they realize humanity's gigantic propensity to error. "Try to do no good," he asserted trenchantly, "and then you won't get into any scrapes."

But it was in his attitude to religion that his duality of mind appeared most significantly. Many people thought he was an atheist. Certainly he talked flippantly about

257

the most holy topics; he seldom went to church himself, and he did not like other people going often; "No, my Lord," he replied to the disconcerted Archbishop of York, who had invited him to attend the evening service, "once is orthodox, twice is puritanical." And he had a horror of pious emotionalism—"Things are coming to a pretty pass," he exclaimed, after listening to an evangelical sermon on the consequences of sin, "when religion is allowed to invade private life." Roman Catholicism, in his view, was insufficiently calm, and he recommended the Church of England on the ground it was the "least meddlesome." Yet the subject of religion exercised over him a strange compelling fascination. For hours he would sit studying the controversies of the early fathers; every new theological work found its way to his shelves, its margins scrawled with his notes. No doubt this was partly due to historical interest. Religion, he once said, had played so prominent a role in human history, that every educated man should investigate it. Perhaps he also found an ironical amusement in contemplating the extraordinary figments of fancy with which, according to his ideas, human beings had seen fit still further to confuse their already perplexed lives. But there was, all the same, a serious side to his religious preoccupations. The imaginative element in him cried out against a purely rationalistic interpretation of the universe. And the mystical strain, stirring always in the hinterland of his consciousness, set him wondering if there was not something in religion after all. Certainly there were things in his experience inexplicable by rationalist theory. If he searched the records of religion long enough, might he not discover an explanation of them—might he not even find grounds for that faith for which, in spite of himself, his spirit yearned? Anyway there was no harm in trying. In a world where all was obscure, the speculations of the theologians had as good a chance of being true as anything else.

For this was the final result of his cogitations; a scepticism more complete, because more considered, even than that of his youth. When the evidence of heart and head, of reason and imagination, contradicted each other at every turn, he could put no certain trust in his judgment. And the opinions of others, so far as he had studied them, provided no more satisfactory solution to the riddle. How could one trust the judgment of beings, the essential condition of whose nature it was to be limited and biased and ignorant? "Neither man nor woman," he noted, "can be worth anything until they have discovered that they are fools. This is the first step towards becoming either estimable or agreeable; and until it be taken there is no hope. The sooner the discovery is made the better, as there is more time and power for taking advantage of it. Sometimes the great truth is found out too late to apply to it any effectual remedy. Sometimes it is never found at all; and these form the desperate and inveterate causes of folly, self-conceit and impertinence."

No, life was an insoluble conundrum; and all that a sensible man could do was to try and get through it with as little unpleasantness to himself, and everyone else, as possible; in private to be considerate and detached, in public to do what little he could to guide the world down its uncharted course with the minimum of friction. This generally involved doing very little. It certainly meant refusing to risk an immediate disturbance for the sake of a problematical future good. As for ultimate truth, the nearest an honest man could hope to get to that, was to be vigilantly faithful to the conclusions of his own reason and experience; not to let his candid impressions be distorted by convention or cowardice or the deceptions of his own vanity. Probably, these personal conclusions were as far from the truth as everything else. But they were the only things of which he had first-hand evidence. Anyway only good could come of speaking one's mind, even if it did shock people. "It is a good thing to surprise," he once said. By shaking others out of their complacency one might make them realize how ill-founded human convictions are.

He reaped the reward of his courage. William got

closer to truth, pierced far deeper into the significance of
things, than the majority of his hustling contemporaries.
All the same his creed was not an inspiriting one. And
there was a strong undercurrent of melancholy in him.
"To those who think," he was fond of quoting, "life is
a comedy, to those who feel a tragedy." William was
far too sensitive not to feel its tragic implications more
often than was comfortable for him. Fits of depression
overtook him, in which he sat silent and remote, overwhelmed by a sense of the barren fleetingness of existence; and even his brightest moods were shot through
by grey streaks of disillusionment. Yet he was not so
unhappy as might have been expected. For one thing
he was no longer at open war with himself. Though
the discordant elements in him were as discordant as
ever, he had given up trying to reconcile them. He had
imposed an armistice on his inner struggle, he had come
to terms with his difficulties. Besides, happiness is an
affair of temperament rather than opinions. And William's temperament was all salt and sunshine. The depression of 1816 was too alien from his spirit to last long;
when the immediate cloud passed, willy-nilly he began
to respond to life again; by the time he was forty-six he
had recovered nearly all his youthful capacity for enjoyment. The world might be a futile place; but how odd
it was, how fascinating, how endlessly full of interest!

By now he had acquired the skill of a life-long hedonist in extracting every drop of pleasure from life that it had to offer. "Lord Melbourne looked as if he enjoyed himself," said a surprised observer who had watched him beaming at some tedious city banquet. "There is nothing Lord Melbourne does not enjoy," was the reply. Along with his pleasure in life went a pleasure in his fellow creatures. Most cynics have a fundamental antipathy to their kind; not so William. "The worst of the present day," he once said to a friend, "is that men hate one another so damnably. For my part I love them all!" This was a slight exaggeration. Arrogant people irritated him profoundly, and pretentious ones still more. "There now, that fellow has been trying for half-an-hour to make me believe he knows a great deal of what he knows nothing," he commented after listening to a literary man holding forth at his table, "we won't have him again." But though he did not love everybody, he liked most and hated none. Himself normal in his tastes, he felt at home with the normal run of humanity; sympathized with their aspirations, shared their pleasures, understood their weaknesses. Perhaps human beings were not very dignified; but then, he did not feel dignified himself. Besides their absurdities and inconsistencies only made them the more entertaining. And if he liked men as a whole, certain individuals among them he loved. Experience had only confirmed the strength of his personal affections. For Emily, for Fred, for his closest friends, he felt an ardent unselfish love that overrode all his deliberately cultivated detachment. Unquenchable beacons of comfort and joy they shone out, radiating a little circle of light in the huge darkness of the universe, warming the shivering heart. Indeed the very paradox of his nature made him a happy man on the whole. A cynic who loved mankind, a sceptic who found life thoroughly worth living, he contrived to face the worthlessness of things, cheerfully enough.

Only there was a chink in the armour of his serenity. It depended too much on keeping in the sun. Since he relied for happiness on the passing joys of pleasure and affection, he must manage his life so that these were always at his disposal. A threat to the amenity of his mode of existence was deeply disturbing to him. As we have seen he was terrified of revolution. And in private life too, he avoided the disagreeable as much as he could. He had a horror of seeing a corpse, for instance. Even in books, he refused to read anything that dealt with the grim or the sordid. Crabbe, he said, degraded everything he touched; and in later years he put aside *Oliver Twist* after one glance. "It is all among workhouses and pickpockets and coffinmakers," he said, "I do not *like* those things: I wish to avoid them. I do not like

263

them in reality and therefore I do not like to see them represented."

Indeed there was a flaw in his philosophy, a radical defect, implicit in this shrinking from the unpleasant. The happiness that is an expression only of an instinctive mood has no certainty of continuance; William's serenity rested on no reasoned foundation, but only on a precariously-adjusted equilibrium. For the present his sanguine temperament was strong enough to provide a counter-weight to the melancholy of his scepticism. But supposing his mood changed, supposing that, stricken by sorrow or by the failure of vitality, he lost his faculty of enjoyment—at once he would be flung into that slough of despond to which his intellectual convictions might logically seem to consign him. Only as long as he kept his balance was he safe; and in a world of chance and catastrophe, at any moment it might begin to waver.

The truth was that William's mature character, like his youthful, was a compromise. In a sense he had made far more of a success of it than most people. For he was that rare phenomenon, a genuinely independent personality. From the turmoil of warring influences which, from cradle to middle age, had fought for possession of him, he had emerged dominated by none, his every opinion the honest conclusion of his own experience; his every utterance and habit, down to the way he ate,

THE FINISHED PRODUCT

and folded his letters, the unqualified expression of his
own individuality. But, though he was enslaved to
nothing else, he was not master of himself. Strong
enough to reject any faith that his own reason did not
think convincing, he had not the strength to form a
faith of his own. His spiritual security was at the mercy
of circumstances.

And the course of his life too. His philosophy hampered his power of action. It was not that he was weak,
as his friends, from Emily down, were always complain-
ing. On the contrary, no one could act more vigorously
once he was convinced he was right. The trouble was
that he was seldom so convinced. He saw every question
from so many sides, most problems seemed to him so
hopeless of solution, that he was generally for doing
nothing at all. Still less could he direct his various actions to a chosen end: he had never made up his mind
as to whether any end was worth achieving. If circumstances should happen to push him into a position of
power, he was perfectly ready to take it on: for men
and their affairs inspired him with far too little respect
for him to shrink from assuming responsibility for them.
But, on the other hand, he did not think it worth while
stirring a finger to mould circumstances to his will. Smiling, indolent, and inscrutable he lay, a pawn in the hands
of fortune.

265

LIST OF AUTHORITIES

The Bessborough Papers.
The British Museum Papers.
The Chatsworth Papers.
The Holland House Papers.
The Lamb Papers, in the possession of Lady Salisbury.
Lord Melbourne's Papers.
The Panshanger Papers.
The Windsor Papers.

AIRLIE, MABELL COUNTESS OF. In Whig Society.
AIRLIE, MABELL COUNTESS OF. Lady Palmerston and Her Times.
ASPINALL, ARTHUR. Lord Brougham and the Whig Party.
BADDELY, SOPHIA. Memoirs.
BERRY, MISS MARY. Extracts from Journal and Correspondence.
BLESSINGTON, COUNTESS OF. Conversations of Lord Byron with the Countess of Blessington.
BROUGHAM, HENRY, IST BARON. Life and Times of Brougham.
BROUGHTON, LORD. Recollections of a Long Life.

LIST OF AUTHORITIES

BURY, LADY CHARLOTTE. Diary illustrative of the times of George IV.

BYRON, LORD. Letters and Journals.

BYRON, LORD. Collected Poems.

CANNING, GEORGE. Some Official Correspondence.

CREEVEY PAPERS.

DALLAS, ROBERT. Recollections of the life of Lord Byron.

D'ARBLAY, MADAME. Diary and Letters.

DUDLEY, JOHN WILLIAM WARD, EARL. Letters to "Ivy."

DUNCKLEY, HENRY. Lord Melbourne.

FONBLANQUE, E. Life and Letters of Albany Fonblanque.

FOSTER, VERE. The Two Duchesses.

FULFORD, R. George IV.

GALT, JOHN. Life of Byron.

GLENBERVIE, SYLVESTER DOUGLAS. Journals.

GODWIN, W. Correspondence.

GREVILLE MEMOIRS.

GUEDALLA, PHILIP. Palmerston.

HALEVY, ELIE. History of the English People in the nineteenth century. 1815–1830.

HAYDON, BENJAMIN. Diaries of.

HAYWARD, ABRAHAM. Sketches of Eminent Statesmen and Writers.

HOLLAND, LORD. Memoirs of the Whig Party during my Time.

HOLLAND, ELIZABETH LADY. Journal 1791–1811.

LIST OF AUTHORITIES

ILCHESTER, EARL OF. Home of the Hollands, 1605–1820.

ILCHESTER, EARL OF. Chronicles of Holland House, 1820–1900.

JENKINS, ELIZABETH. Lady Caroline Lamb.

JERDAN, WILLIAM. Autobiography.

KEMBLE, FANNY. Records of a Girlhood.

LAMB, LADY CAROLINE. Glenarvon.

LEE, DR. ROBERT. Extracts from Diary.

LE MARCHANT. Memoirs of Viscount Althorp.

LENNOX. Life and Letters of Sarah.

LEVESON-GOWER, GRANVILLE. Private Correspondence.

LIEVEN, PRINCESS. Letters of.

LYTTELTON, SARAH SPENCER, LADY. Correspondence.

LYTTON, ROBERT, 1ST EARL. Life of Edward Bulwer Lytton.

MACAULAY, LORD. Critical and Historical Essays.

MCCULLAGH-TORRENS, W. T. Memoirs of Melbourne.

MARKHAM, VIOLET. Paxton and the Bachelor Duke.

MAYNE, E. C. Byron.

MAYNE, E. C. Life and Letters of Anne Isabella, Lady Byron.

MEDWIN, THOMAS. Conversation of Byron at Pisa.

MORGAN, LADY. Memoirs, autobiography, diaries and correspondence.

MOORE, THOMAS. Memoirs, journal and correspondence.

NEWMAN, BERTRAM. Lord Melbourne.

QUENNELL, PETER. Byron: the Years of Fame.

LIST OF AUTHORITIES

RUSSELL, G. W. E. Collections and Recollections.

SADLEIR, MICHAEL. Bulwer and his Wife.

SANDERS, LLOYD C. The Holland House Circle.

SELWYN, GEORGE A. His Letters and his Life.

SHELLEY, FRANCES WINCKLEY, LADY. Diary of.

SICHEL, WALTER. Sheridan.

SMILES, SAMUEL. A Publisher and His Friends.

STOKES, HUGH. The Devonshire House Circle.

TEMPERLEY, H. W. V. Life of Canning.

TREVELYAN, G. M. British History in the nineteenth century.

TREVELYAN, G. M. Lord Grey of the Reform Bill.

VICTORIA, QUEEN. Letters.

WALPOLE, HORACE. Letters.

WALPOLE, SIR SPENCER. History of England from the conclusion of the great war in 1815.

WALPOLE, SIR SPENCER. Life of Lord John Russell.

WHATELY, E. J. Life and Correspondence of Archbishop Whately.

WILBERFORCE, R. I. Life of William Wilberforce.

WILSON, HARRIETTE. Memoirs.

WRAXALL, SIR NATHANIEL. Posthumous Memoirs of his own Time.

INDEX

271

INDEX

Chatham, Lord, 57
Childe Harold, 148
Clark, Mrs. Ann, 130
Clive, Kitty, 10
Coke, Sir Edward, 139
Coleraine, Lord, 27, 31
Cowper, Countess, *see* Lamb, Emily
—— Lord, 212
Crabbe, George, 9, 263
Damer, Mrs., 31
Devonshire, Georgiana, Duchess of, 10, 11, 29, 31, 53, 55, 58, 60-63, 89, 102
—— William Cavendish, 5th Duke, 6, 11, 29, 58, 61
—— William George Spencer Cavendish, 6th Duke, 232
Devonshire House, 52, 54, 58-62, 72, 100, 108
Duncannon, Lady, 240
Duncombe, Thomas, 209
Egremont, George Wyndham, 3rd Earl of, 7, 28-30, 33, 35, 39, 42, 67, 84
Eldon, Lord, 208
Ellenborough, Lord, 130
Eton, 35, 43-44, 46, 47
Fénelon, 256
Fitzgerald, Miss Pamela, 11
Fitzherbert, Mrs., 53
Foster, Caroline, 112
—— Lady Elizabeth, 11, 58, 61-62
Fox, Charles James, 13, 31, 49,

52, 56, 68, 101, 102, 125, 126
Foxites, 126, 132, 195, 208
French Revolution, 124, 128
Gainsborough, Thomas, 17
Garter, Order of, 251
George III, 54, 122, 125, 137
George IV (as Prince of Wales), 30, 31, 33, 35, 36, 38, 53, 54, 57, 84, 100, 137, 138, 204, 207, 215
Gifford, William, 229
Glasgow University, 65
Glenarvon, 188-193, 214
Gloucester, Duke of, 100
Goddard, Dr., 241
Godwin, William, 32, 217, 223, 228
Granville, Harriet, Lady, 32, 181, 216
—— Lord, 63, 92, 180
Grenvillites, 126, 132, 208
Grey, Charles, Earl, 11, 30, 121, 124, 126, 208
Haggard, Mr., 220
Hammond, Mr., 93
Hare, Mr., 31
Harley family, 11
Hartington, Lord, 90, 95, 167
Heathcote, Lady, 173, 186
Hertford constituency, 86, 209
Hogarth, William, 17
Holland, Elizabeth Vassall, Lady, 55-58, 67, 69, 100, 135, 144, 145, 147, 189
—— Henry Richard Fox, Lord,

272

83-85; his religious views, 83, 257-260; enters Parliament, 86; his courtship and marriage to Caroline Ponsonby, 86, 89-99; his yearly allowance, 90-91; the birth of a son, 99; social life, 100; instructs Caroline, 103; a rift in his married happiness, 104, 109-118; Parliament and politics, 119-122, 127-140; his view of revolution, 128; offered a post in the administration, 136; the Prince of Wales offers him a place in the Cabinet, 138; decides not to stand in the 1812 election, 140; the wreck of his married life, 141, 143-148; his wife's affair with Byron, 162-166, 176-178; goes to Ireland, 166; his devotion to his wife during her hysteria, 167-168, 176, 179-181; in Paris, 180-181; a judicial separation suggested, 187, 192-193; his wife's novel *Glenarvon*, 191-193; a reconciliation with his wife, 192-193; re-enters the House of Commons, 194-200; continues a stagnant political course, 203-207; accepted as a member of the inner group of Whig leaders, 207; George IV prophesies that one day he will be Prime Minister, 207; his laxity in his attendance at the House, 209; retires from the contest for Hertford, 209-210; his literary work, 210; his mother's death, 212; his sister Emily's devotion to him, 213; his married life from 1816-25, 226-231; again decides on a separation, 231-236; takes an official appointment in Ireland, 237; his wife's illness and death, 239-243; his intellectual development and the development of his character, 244-248; his appearance in middle age, 248; his unconventional habits, 248-249; his conversation, 250; his cynically realistic view of life, 252-257; his political outlook, 257; his tenderness of heart, 257; his attitude to religion, 257-261; his temperament, 261-265

Melbourne House, 31, 32, 35, 52, 53, 54, 99, 100, 137, 144, 188, 216, 217, 242

Milbanke, Annabella, 169, 185

—— Elizabeth, *see* Melbourne, Viscountess

—— Sir Ralph, 27

Millar, Professor, 65-67

Moore, Tom, 52, 142, 210

INDEX